To all who are today in a difficult relationship,
and wish for better days.
May God bless you.

Contents

CONTENTS

ACKNOWLEDGMENTS

BYRON WILLIAMSON, president of Integrity Publishers: For your vision and partnership in publishing. You believe in the process of writing and are a leader in thinking about ways to reach people with books.

Joey Paul, publisher of Integrity: For adding such value to writing and publishing. Your support and rich background have been invaluable.

Rob Birkhead, Integrity's senior vice president, marketing: For your creativity and ability to convey ideas through the visual process. Your work is appreciated.

Sealy Yates, my agent: for being "for" me all these years of writing, and being a pioneer in helping people find God's grace through publishing.

Jeana Ledbetter, my literary representative: for catching the vision for this book early, and providing perspective on its creation.

Anita Palmer, my editor: for your competency and care in restructuring thoughts into words that communicate best what should be said.

Dr. Henry Cloud, my friend and partner: for your involvement in the thinking behind the book, and your years of service to God in his calling to help people find him.

ACKNOWLEDGMENTS

Kris Bearss, Editorial Director at Integrity: for your concern and conscientiousness that the written word be accessible and clear to the reader.

Maureen Price and the Cloud-Townsend Resources staff: Thanks to Jodi Coker, Kevin Doherty, Belinda Falk, Kris Patton, and Raul Peña for your care, your dedication, and your values that have made so much of a difference.

The staff of Cloud-Townsend Clinic: Dr. John Barrett, Dr. Sharon Bultsma, Laura Crutchfield, Dr. Fran Rodenburg, Brett Veltman, and Josh Wilson, for your training and heart in helping those who need to find healing, to experience it.

Steve Arterburn, Mike Marino, and the staff of New Life Ministries: Paul Barnes, Jamie Clark, Jo Crisp, Maureen Fraser, Sue Haffely, Steve Lee, Terry McIntosh, Karen Mendoza, Dianne Nelson, Larry Sonnenburg, and Lisa Voyen, for your support and commitment to using radio and media as a positive way to help people.

Mike Coleman, president of Integrity Media, Inc.: for your leadership and engagement in beginning a publishing arm which could help others grow in Christ.

The attendees of Monday Night Solutions at Mariners Church, Irvine, California: for your desire to grow relationally, spiritually, and emotionally.

Drs. Bruce Narramore, John Carter, and Phil Sutherland: for helping me learn character diagnostics at a deep level.

The faculty of Dallas Theological Seminary: for providing me with the tools to understand scriptural thought.

Tom and Martha McCall and Ted Trubenbach: for your years of safe and sane personal support.

Denis Beausejour: for your involvement in my life beyond ministry.

Acknowledgments

Dr. Bob Bey, John and Laurie Carpenter, Chuck Fay, and Dr. Eric Prouty: for helping me not to forget the right side of my brain.

My wife, Barbi, and our sons, Ricky and Benny: for being the best family I could ask for.

Introduction:
Have Buttons, Will Push

L ET'S BEGIN WITH A LITTLE REALITY CHECK. Are you in a relationship with someone that often results in you feeling significant amounts of the following?

- Frustration?
- Helplessness?
- Fear?
- Alienation and isolation?
- Anxiety?
- Out of control?
- Unloved?
- Guilt?

- Confusion?

- Anger?

This is not a complete list by any means. But if you find yourself here, it may convey that something in this relationship causes significant problems for you, and perhaps for others as well. It is as if aspects of that person's behavior, words, or attitudes have the power and capacity to change your own mood, your happiness, and even your quality of life.

It could certainly be that these reactions are more about you than the other person. That is always something to check out, for example, by seeing if safe and sane people have similar reactions to this person, or by asking others for feedback about your own style of relating. But if it is true that the person is, in objective reality, doing lots of crazy-making or even destructive things in your relationship, you may be dealing with a *button-pusher*.

A button-pusher is someone who causes many negative reactions in his relationships. There are two parts to the equation: the button-pusher's crazy-making tendencies, plus your own vulnerabilities to him or her. The material in this book has been designed to give you the tools to not only understand your situation, but also to develop an approach to the relationship to both influence that difficult person to change in positive ways, and help you change and grow also. Let's look at some examples from life that can flesh out the picture.

THE DINNER FROM MISERY

My wife, Barbi, said to me one evening, "Linda and Jim invited us to dinner. Let's do it." I was up for it. I liked Linda. I had never met her husband, Jim, but dinner sounded OK to me. Calls were placed and plans made, and within a couple of weeks we were at their home.

As we talked over dinner, I liked Linda even more. She was warm, intelligent, and funny. She was easy to get to know, and was one of those people who naturally reaches out and puts people at ease.

Jim, however, was another matter. While he did seem to make an effort to get to know us, it was sort of a bumpy ride. Jim just said and did things that made it very difficult to be in the same room with him for any extended period of time.

For example, when Linda was telling us how they met, Jim interrupted her in mid-sentence.

"Cryin' out loud, Linda, tell the story right," he said. "It wasn't *that* restaurant; it was the Italian one. Here's what really happened." Then he simply finished the story from his own point of view, which positioned Linda as the goofy klutz and himself as the good guy.

It was a little uncomfortable. I felt bad for Linda, but then I thought, *Maybe that's just their style as a couple. He takes over somewhat, but maybe she doesn't need the limelight, it doesn't bug her, and it's harmless.* I didn't quite understand how that particular style would come out so quickly with us, a couple they didn't know, but I figured maybe they were just comfortable with us. I found myself trying to give Jim the benefit of the doubt, being aware of all the things I have done in social settings with my wife that have not been welcomed by her.

But the truth became evident when I snuck a look at Linda's face. She looked hurt but, at the same time, resigned. Apparently this was a pretty familiar scenario for her.

The evening got even more bizarre. Once, Jim got a call on his cell phone when we were in the living room talking, and he proceeded to talk, with us sitting there, to a business colleague using conversational volume levels that preempted our own conversation. It was the kind of situation in which he would make a point with the caller, and then smile and look at us for validation as if to say, *We're all having a good time with this call, huh?* Linda looked pretty miserable, but she didn't say anything, so I didn't either. It went on for a while, then the call ended and we resumed our conversation.

Later that night, after coffee and dessert, Barbi and I offered to help with the dishes, and Linda agreed. The dinner had been a lot of work for her, and she looked a little tired. Jim said to me, "Let me show you the new entertainment center—it's a killer system."

Linda said, "OK, go ahead, we'll clean up."

I said, "No, it's OK, it won't take long. I'll help too."

Jim said, "Come on, come on, you won't believe this setup."

I looked at Linda and she waved us off. Barbi and she began cleaning up. Barbi looked at me as if to say, *Let's roll with it.* So I went to the family room.

Jim did have an amazing entertainment center. Since I had a beginner's understanding of these matters, I was interested. But after a few minutes, I could see that this was becoming a very long and very technical lecture, far above my head and interest level. It went on and on and on. I tried to be a good sport and hang in there, though I could feel my eyes glazing over at times. But I was pretty relieved when he ran down.

At the end of the night, we thanked the couple for having us over and got ready to leave. Out of the blue, Jim said, "I've got to show you guys how we're going to remodel the house. Take a minute and get the tour." We were already late for the babysitter, so I said, "Thanks, but we've got to go. Maybe next time."

Jim said, "Come on, it'll just be a sec. We've got some great plans."

I was starting to get annoyed with the whole evening, so I said, a little more firmly, "No, really, we've really got to scram, I'm sorry."

Jim said, "Oh, come on, guys."

Linda intervened, "Honey, they've really got to go, OK?"

Jim said, "I get it, too good for us, huh? OK, be that way, see if I care, ha ha." It was one of those statements officially labeled as *this is a joke* but you know the person is, underneath it all, bugged with you.

Barbi and I finally escaped to our car and debriefed about the night on the way home. She had had similar reactions to Jim. She thought he was a nice guy at heart, but that he would be very difficult to be around. We joked a little about how long the dinner had been for us, saying that now we needed an evening out to recover from that evening out.

But the upshot of our experience was, more than anything, a feeling of *poor Linda*. We both were drawn to her and felt bad for her. She was really a good person, and, with Jim, she obviously had some problems on her hands. We had to be around him only for a dinner; she was faced with his attitudes all the time.

And the reality was that we knew that we wouldn't be spending a lot more time with them as a couple. It would probably be more just Barbi and Linda getting together. With time as tight as it is in life, you just want to carve out get-togethers with people that you both can connect with. And that was sad for me because I liked Linda, and also because I figured that our evening with Linda and Jim was something that had happened with others a lot. It was likely that there weren't a lot of couples that could spend sustained time with Jim.

There were lots of losses in this situation. I was losing out with Linda, she was losing out with others, and at some level, Jim was losing out on the possibility of having people around him who could help him change.

I Love Mom, But . . .

Then there are more serious situations of this same sort, which I often see in the consulting room. For example, I worked with Tony, a professional man in his thirties whose mother, Evelyn, was such a destructive person that his own marriage, as well as his emotional condition, was in jeopardy. Lest you think this is a far reach, it happens more than people might think. Here are the facts.

Evelyn was a severe alcoholic in denial. She lived alone but within driving distance of Tony and his wife, Jen's, home. She would call several times daily, and at all hours of the night, begging Tony to come visit her either because she was lonely, or because she felt she was in a crisis. Sometimes she truly was, as when she would accidentally set fire to things or fall down and hurt herself. She refused to move into an assisted living situation, and was one of those people whose condition is not quite severe enough to be involuntarily placed in a safer setting. She had never been involved in a supportive community setting, so her "only friend" was Tony. Her dependency on him was immense.

When she visited his home, she would scare his kids with her ravings. He couldn't have other guests over at the same time because she would be wildly inappropriate. There were times when he had had to call the police to find her when she ran out of the house crying over an imagined slight from Tony or Jen.

When Tony came to see me, he was in the throes of guilt, resentment, and burnout. He drove to see her as much as he could, but it was never enough. He tried reasoning with her, being firm with her, ignoring her, and getting her to make friends, all to no avail. Though at first Jen tried to be supportive, after several years she had had it with the chaos her mother-in-law was causing and had begun to blame Tony for not standing up to her. She was talking about him moving out so that she and the kids could have some sort of normalcy. It was one of those her-or-me scenarios.

It took Tony a lot of work to improve things with Evelyn, and also with Jen. He was in such conflict: he loved his mom, he was frustrated with her attitudes, and yet he was afraid she would fall apart. However, the work he did and the structures we set up—which are based on the principles in this book—improved the situation a great deal.

Making the Choice

Though Tony's situation was very different than Linda's, they both had something in common: *someone important to them was affecting their lives in very negative ways.* They were not dealing with a stranger or an enemy, but a person with whom they hoped they would have a good, long, and meaningful relationship.

I heard recently from friends who also knew Jim and Linda, who I had not seen for a long time. They said that Jim had not changed, and that Linda was still burdened by his ways. My friends also told me that to date, Linda had not, to their knowledge, tried any sorts of approaches to address her husband's behavior. Perhaps she had tried some things, but whatever she tried didn't work. Maybe she blamed herself for Jim. Or maybe she figured things weren't bad enough to try to find solutions. During the time I was with Jim and Linda, I didn't think their condition warranted professional counseling. From what I could see, there were things Linda could do—which this book teaches—that would help the situation a great deal.

Tony's situation, on the other hand, had been obviously out of control. Because he was truly and undeniably at the end of his rope, in a situation that was extreme, he needed a more formal setting to implement these principles.

There is an irony here: the less severe situation did not improve, but the worse one got better. Tony told me that he felt he had no choice. He had to do something. I reflected on the scripture that says, "Blessed are those who hunger and thirst for righteousness, for they will be filled" (Matthew 5:6). I was glad that Tony took his big step, and I hoped that someday Linda would find the right answers also.

WHO IS YOUR BUTTON-PUSHER?

This is probably not a rocket-scientist question for most of us to answer. You can likely relate to having a person, or people, like Jim or Evelyn in your life. Your button-pusher may not have the same attitudes and behaviors these individuals showed, but he or she is, at some level, difficult to like, love, be with, or work with. There is something in your button-pusher that makes life and love harder for you when you are with him. His ways can be mild, or moderate, or severe.

It is important to realize that, most of the time, your button-pusher is also someone you care about. That is, the person has some weight, meaning, and importance in your life. You probably would much prefer working things out than leaving the relationship, because you value the good things he does have. But your button-pusher's character and patterns make that very difficult.

Joined at the hip. Your button-pusher is part of your life and matters to you. That is a prerequisite. She can be a spouse, a parent, someone you are dating. Or he can be someone you work with, a neighbor, or a friend. Generally, it is someone connected to you by blood (family relationships), love (romance and friendships), or money (work relationships). Blood, love, and money are powerful forces that create a bond between people. They aren't bad things; in fact, they are part of the glue that holds life, culture, and civilization together. They are just categories to be able to understand your relationships.

There are all sorts of button-pushing people, and they can be found in many arenas of your life. Here's a sample:

- The controlling boss who micromanages people
- The dependent adult child who constantly drains you
- The detached husband who will not communicate
- The blaming wife who will not take responsibility for her side of things
- The victim who wants you to rescue her from all the perpetrators
- The spiritualizing friend who preaches instead of listening
- The unpredictable spouse who is clingy one minute and pushing away the next
- The irresponsible boyfriend who can't be depended on
- The deceptive person who turns the truth into white or black lies
- The self-absorbed mom who turns everything to herself
- The moody co-worker whose ups and downs control the work environment
- The alcoholic or drug addict who causes chaos in others' lives
- The rageaholic dad who has everyone walking on eggshells
- The gossiping relative who causes divisions in the family

The list could go on and on.

So What Are My Buttons?

However, for there to be a problem, there must be a button inside you that is being pushed. That is, this person has a very real and specific effect on your life, emotions, and attitudes. He "gets to you" in ways that others don't.

The range of reactions you may have is almost endless, but there are a few more or less universal ones.

Disconnection

While you may want to establish some closeness, empathy, or intimacy with your button-pusher, it does not happen. This may be because he does not respond to you and withdraws himself emotionally. *I cannot reach him* is a common experience. Or it may be because his actions are not consistent with his words, so you feel confused. Sometimes it is due to the fact that you have to pull away from any closeness because the relationship is unsafe for you at this time. A person who is with a button-pusher will often sense that *he doesn't "get" me*; that is, he doesn't enter my world and experience. Or it may seem that your feelings don't matter to him and his choices. This sort of disconnection can cause deep feelings of isolation, alienation, and loneliness.

Diminishing of Love

Often, the person feels that the love she has felt for the individual is waning. If the situation involves a spouse or dating relationship, she doesn't feel that she is "in love." Or she doesn't experience the warmth and affection inside her toward that person that she did, or would like to. It is as if all the crazy things the button-pusher is and does are beginning to destroy the affection she has. Sometimes, the person even feels that the love inside has died and can never be reborn or rebuilt.

Actually, this can be a helpful sign for someone in a relationship with a difficult person. If love has diminished, then it indicates that the person did have a meaningful place in your mind, heart, and life. He mattered. And a person who has mattered to you stands a better chance of being re-established with the right processes than someone you never deeply cared about.

Powerlessness

You may also feel that you can't do anything to change the situation, the button-pusher's behavior, or the relationship. You may have tried talking, reasoning, inviting, or threatening, and nothing seems to make a difference. This describes a power problem, in which all choices and movement seem to be owned by the button-pusher rather than being shared by both parties.

In a good relationship, both people share responsibility, initiative, problem solving, and choices in a more or less equal way. But in a button-pushing relationship, the individual often feels helpless, impotent, and frustrated. He or she wants and desires good things to happen but has found no way to improve things. This book will deal specifically with using the power and choices that you have, which you may not be aware that you possess, or which you have been afraid to bring into leverage in the relationship.

Bringing Out Your Worst

When you are with your button-pusher, often you may find that you have feelings, thoughts, behaviors, and words that you don't like about yourself. It is as if her issues trigger your darker self. You may find yourself angrier than you would like to be, overwhelmed with sadness, or withdrawn from relationships. Sometimes you may even be revengeful or mean, playing payback in the relationship.

This is a telling sign of a troublesome relationship. God designed us so that good relationships should draw out and encourage the best in us: love, care, and the ability to give freely of yourself. When you don't like the person you are when you're around your button-pusher, it is time to make some changes.

Other Relationships Affected

The button-pushing person often has the power to influence how you handle your other attachments. You may find, for example, that you have become obsessed and too focused on the troublesome relationship.

Have you ever had the weird experience at lunch with someone when it seems that there is a third party there who is not physically present? Your friend is so obsessed on the problem person that that troublemaker might as well pick up the lunch tab. That is a clear signal that the difficult person is running things, and, while she needs to be loved, she must be fired from that role.

Loss of Hope

Perhaps the most serious effect of being with a button-pusher is that people begin losing hope that anything will change. They think that things will always be this bad, and that they should resign themselves to this existence or somehow leave it.

This is so serious because we all need hope. Hope is what fuels us to strive for a better life and future. When hope decreases, we give up. A wise axiom says, "Hope deferred makes the heart sick, but a longing fulfilled is a tree of life" (Proverbs 13:12).

Certainly there are those who use their freedom to resist any sort of change; no one could deny that. However, my experience is that much of the time, *someone in the button-pusher's life did not possess either the information, the resources, or the courage needed to help make change*. Either she didn't know what to do, or he didn't have the support, or they were too afraid to make effective changes. We will talk about establishing substantive hope in the pages to come.[1]

WHAT RELATIONSHIPS SHOULD GIVE YOU

However, sometimes people who have had a button-pusher in their life for a long time have forgotten, or never knew, what a good relationship should bring to them. They don't know what "normal" is, in the same way a fish doesn't know it is wet. So it is important to understand the value and nature of relationships.

Human connections are one of the greatest things that anyone can experience in life. The rich man who is without them is impoverished; the poor man who has them is wealthy. God himself is relational at the core of his being: He is love (1 John 4:16). And he designed us to be in, depend on, thrive on, and grow from relationships.

Look at your relationships as the "delivery system" for so many of the good things we need in life. We need love, safety, grace, warmth, encouragement, truth and feedback, forgiveness, and so much more. These elements of life make life full, meaningful, purposeful, and enjoyable.

Without solid, long-lasting connections, we suffer at many levels of life. The research indicates that people with unhealthy or few good relationships have more medical and psychological problems, and generally experience a deprived quality of life.

Take a moment to compare your healthy relationships with what you have with the button-pusher, not in a condemning way, but to get a picture of what life could be like otherwise. You and that person were designed to mutually assist and support each other through the avenues of life to become the people that God intended and designed.

This is not to say that even good connections don't have their valleys; they all do. But when both people are on the path to growth, they have developed several capacities which cover up and resolve problems. They own their part in the problems; they let the other person know their heart, and strive to know the other's heart; they take responsibility for helping the relationship grow; they forgive, change, and move on.

How Can He "Get To Me?"

Often, someone in a button-pushing relationship will come to me and say, "Why do I let her get to me like I do? Why can't I just get past what she says and let it slide off my back?" These questions imply that something is wrong with you if you have negative reactions to the individual, that you should not let her matter to you as much as she does.

This book will help you be *less reactive* to that person, and that is important. You need to be in control of yourself and your responses. We will help you learn to deal better with verbal attacks, irresponsibility, withdrawal, and the like. That will help you enormously in dealing effectively with her in achieving change.

When you care, you are vulnerable. At the same time, however, understand this: *The fact that others can affect you deeply may say some very good things about who you are*. If you are able to care about someone else so much that they make you feel crazy and powerless, you have the capacity for love and attachment, and that is a wonderful thing. This capacity is one of the most important aspects of what being alive and human are all about. If you can feel, care, be vulnerable, get frustrated, love, and hate, then you are not dead inside but alive.

"Normal" Pain

I was working with Cathy and Dave, a dating couple who were considering marriage but were having problems. The short version is that he was very self-involved, and she was getting tired of having to stroke his ego constantly and never having him ask her how she was feeling. Dave's experience was that things were basically OK. He was going to counseling to humor Cathy. In his mind, his biggest problem was that Cathy was asking too much, and if she'd back off, they'd both be happy.

Cathy wasn't perfect, but I sided with her on this one. Dave was pretty self-centered. And the fact that she experienced more loneliness, need, and powerlessness than Dave did really bothered her.

She said to me, "I should be more like Dave. What I do really doesn't get to him."

I told her, "Forget that. If you, Cathy, were as narcissistic as you are, Dave, no one would be working on this relationship."

I was speaking to both of them in the room at the same time. Dave didn't like to hear that, but eventually he began to see that Cathy's pain was normal and his lack of it was abnormal. He did get to work on his self-absorption. It took some time. In fact, they eventually broke up over it all. Ultimately, however, Dave worked through a lot, and he ended up marrying someone else, as did Cathy.

If you experience the pain of a struggling relationship, you are in good company, for God himself is the same way. He cares deeply and emotionally for us, and, in some mysterious fashion, we can "push his buttons." Read the turmoil in God's heart when he was dealing with some difficult people:

> How can I give you up, Ephraim?
> How can I hand you over, Israel?
> How can I make you like Admah?
> How can I set you like Zeboiim?

My heart churns within Me;
My sympathy is stirred. (Hosea 11:8 NKJV)

It's a striking picture: an all-powerful Creator becoming so vulnerable to us that he churns within. His might and strength notwithstanding, he can be affected inside by those he loves.

To not let someone matter to you, annoy you, or "get to you" at all is to be disconnected from what is important. Those who never allow another to affect them have something wrong with them. They may be emotionally disconnected from their own hearts, due to some past significant relational damage. They may have given up on relationships and simply withdrawn into busyness, work, or even addictions. Or, like Dave, they may have a problem with self-centeredness to the point that other people exist as objects, not as individuals. Whatever the reason, it is not a good thing.

Elie Wiesel, the great Jewish Holocaust survivor and Nobel Peace Prize winner, said it this way: "The opposite of love is not hate; it's indifference."

The Christian thinker C. S. Lewis wrote in a similar vein:

> To love at all is to be vulnerable. . . . The alternative to tragedy, or at least to the risk of tragedy, is damnation. The only place outside Heaven where you can be perfectly safe from all the dangers and perturbations of love is Hell. (From *The Four Loves*)

So turning to stone—becoming impassive or unfeeling—is not the answer. That is not where life or love reside. Rather, one of the most important goals for you in this book *is to learn to care deeply for the other person and for the relationship, but at the same time to be free to respond in healthy and effective ways to his behaviors so that you can bring about change.*

Introduction

Hurt versus Harm

There is a difference, however, between hurt, which involves pain, and injury, which involves harm. You may feel pain and negative emotions as a result of being with your button-pusher. That is simply the price of the course, the price of love. But allowing the person's nonresponsiveness to injure you in some way is not good for you or him. Your relationship should bruise you sometimes, but it shouldn't send you to the ER. That must be dealt with, and this book will show you how to do that.

Those who matter the most can bother you the most. Simply put, *your button-pusher matters to you a great deal for some reason, most likely a good one*. When people matter to us, we tend to give them access to our inner selves that we don't give to others.

It is important to understand that this person can affect you in ways that others cannot. The range of ways that your button-pusher can influence you is enormous and far ranging. He can (or perhaps he used to) bring you moments of closeness, intimacy, passion, fun, and spiritual union. At the same time, his darker sides can influence you toward frustration, disconnection, powerlessness, sadness, and feeling unloved. The intensity of his effect on you is directly proportional to the depth of the attachment you have for him.

In other words, *if your button-pusher didn't matter so much to you, he would not be able to "get to you" to such an extent*. The checker at the grocery store may be cranky, but her bad mood can't affect you like this person can.

Not long ago, I was ordering a burger at a fast food restaurant. The man taking my order seemed impatient and curt with me. Sometimes in these situations, I will say something to the person, or to the management if it's severe enough. I was a waiter for many years in grad school, so I have a thing about decent service. In this case I didn't say anything, thinking, *Oh well, maybe it's my percep-*

tion, and he has a tough job anyway. Forget it. He's probably someone else's button-pusher.

Later that evening, one of my sons seemed a little impatient and curt with me. Immediately I lit into him, saying something like, "This sort of disrespect is unacceptable, and if you ever want to see your CD collection again, you'll change your tune!" It wasn't a high point in my fathering life. My son had committed a misdemeanor, and I was treating it like a felony. Now, I don't consider my kids to be button-pushers. (They may not be able to say the same thing about me!) But the stories illustrate this point: *Those who matter most to you will affect you the most.*

Choosing from Brokenness

There are also some not-so-healthy reasons why we let a button-pusher get to us. Sometimes, we are wanting something from them that they can't provide, or that we shouldn't be asking from them.

We choose people for various reasons, some sound and some crazy. Basically, there are things you want from the other person that you value, whether or not you are aware of it. Some good things to desire are companionship, depth, acceptance, maturity, structure, responsibility, and spirituality. These are the elements of very good relationships.

However, there is another list that can be problematic. It is not that these things are bad, but that it may not be appropriate to ask for them from that person. For example, some people who are afraid of conflict will, instead of working on learning to argue well, find an aggressive, argumentative person to do the job for them. Or someone who feels unloved will look for someone to give her grace and compassion 24/7, uninterrupted by truth and honesty. Or someone who is unfocused and scattered will seek out a highly organized, compulsive person.

While it's good to look for strengths in a person, beware when you want that person to fill the deficits and broken parts of yourself. It is pretty much a guarantee that one of two things will result. You will be frustrated because they can't give you enough of what you need, or they will become controlling, withdrawn, or unloving because they either feel like a parent, or in worse scenarios, as if they have license to do whatever they want with you.

When you look at it this way, it makes sense that the button-pusher can tweak your insides and upset you. He is in charge of an important part of you that you need help on. This is a dangerous position to be in, and this book will help you get out of that sort of dependency on the wrong person and into dependency in the right places.

CREATING HOPE THAT IS REAL

The hope here, that things can change, is not based on wishful thinking. In the many books I have read concerning difficult people, there is a lot of good information that describes the types of people who make life hard. But often, the solutions convey a sense of hopelessness. The idea seems to be that these people will never change, so change yourself, or leave and get out of it, or just learn to cope with a bad situation. Some sources give hope for minimal change, and that's about it: *These types of people are stuck in their attitudes; they rarely change*, they say.

People Can Change

For example, just the other day I was listening to one of the many counseling call-in talk radio programs. The caller's problem was that her husband was uncommunicative and somewhat irresponsible. The counselor said something like, "That's a character problem;

those don't change. Your only two options are to decide if you can live with the way he is, or leave the relationship."

I was really concerned when I heard that statement. It is so not true that people with character problems don't change. Without denying that things can certainly be very difficult, I believe that the Bible, reality, research, and my own experiences all come together to provide more hope than that. Difficult, button-pushing people can and do change, in deep and long-lasting ways, all the time. I have seen it, and many others have witnessed and been a part of it.

God has been in the business of changing difficult people for eons. The Apostle Paul, one of the chief writers of the Bible, said that before God transformed him, he himself had been "the worst of sinners" (1 Timothy 1:16).

Look at it in this light: *in a way, your button-pusher is outmanned and outgunned.* God has engineered things to put various sorts of influences in your button-pusher's life so that he will aright himself and move in the right paths. There is a lot you can do, and that God can do through you: "I know that you can do all things; no plan of yours can be thwarted" (Job 42:2). We are talking about Omnipotence personified on your side! There's a great deal of value here. And the seven resources for change that we will present in section 3 were designed to surround your difficult person with love, truth, reality, and a number of other things. There may be no guarantees of change, as people can still choose poorly. But it is good to have the right and full perspective here.

Crafting a Vision

Being an agent of change will take some work, time, and energy. You will need to experience hope that what you want to see happen in your relationship with your button-pusher can actually happen. Hope that is based on reality and not wishful thinking will give you a vision that will help carry you through as you go through the steps involved.

Though you will learn how to craft your own individual vision for your particular situation in chapter 4, the general idea is this: *that the quality of your relationship improves because the other person is taking responsibility to change his troublesome behaviors and attitudes.*

It seems simple, but all the elements you will need are there. You ultimately are looking for an improved relationship with your button-pusher. That may mean more intimacy, more freedom, more sharing of responsibilities, less criticism, or less control. But since the other person's issues are like a giant traffic jam in your connection, they block all the good things you want in the relationship. Your hope is that as the person "gets it" and begins to take ownership of what his contribution is, then begins to change, the jam gets unblocked and the connection resumes at a traffic flow that distributes all the good you are wanting in that relationship.

In my counseling, speaking, and personal life, I have seen changes and growth take place in so many ways.

- The controlling boss begins to lighten up and give people slack.

- The dependent adult child grows up and establishes a life of his own.

- The detached husband begins to open up emotionally.

- The blaming wife apologizes and becomes concerned about her part.

- The victim becomes stronger and more autonomous.

- The spiritualizing friend gets real about life.

- The irresponsible boyfriend becomes more reliable.

- The deceptive person becomes more honest.

- The self-absorbed mom learns to be concerned about others' experiences.

- The alcoholic or drug addict gets help and becomes a contributing part of life.

- The rageaholic dad becomes kinder and less reactive.

- The gossiping relative sets limits on her tongue.

Note that we are not talking about perfection here; if you have idealistic or perfectionistic leanings, toss them out the window if you want success with your button-pusher. That can ruin your relationship. You are looking for improvement, perhaps a lot of it; but be satisfied with that, not perfection.

Leaving Is for Wimps (with Some Exceptions)

It can be a little overwhelming: when you see in print all the ways your button-pusher can affect you, and how that happens, it makes sense to wonder if it's worth keeping the relationship or if maybe you should end it. *Why put up with this? Why not cut the ties and move on?* There certainly is no question that there really are times a relationship should be over, which will be presented in this book.

Also, sometimes people have been hurt in very bad ways because they didn't leave when they should have left. If you are in a truly dangerous position, no one in his right mind would tell you to stay in jeopardy. This may mean leaving the home or separating for a while in order to safely deal with the problems. It may not mean leaving permanently, however. As we will see later, there can be great benefit in a separation when there is a structured plan that addresses the issues.

Having said that, however, in my experience *the great majority of people give up too soon on their button-pusher.* They have a limited repertoire of responses, none of which are effective, and the situation sometimes even escalates, which gives them fewer options. So they give up in hopelessness. This book will provide strategies and ideas that can help the situation turn around. So for now, let's say that, with some exceptions, stay in the relationship, but in a different way than you have been. Face the issues, learn the skills, and let's get to work.

Remember also that *you have an investment in the relationship.* She is an important person in your life. You have most likely spent many, many hours, days, or years being involved with her. A relationship is an investment of your time, energy, and soul. Though it may be crazy-making today, it may be too great a cost to leave if there were some things you could do to improve it. Too many people dump their stocks and then find that the company rallies later.

Love Doesn't Leave

On a deeper level, it's important to understand that *the nature of love is to stay.* Love relationships (as opposed to task or business relationships) are designed to develop, grow, and mature over time as the two individuals also grow. Love is about things getting better the longer you stay, not worse. Your button-pusher is not someone who you would easily and casually leave. You are intertwined at many levels. It is worth the trouble to take a look at ways that the love you had, and want, can be revived and reborn.

We live in a day and a culture in which relationships are seen sometimes as quite disposable and easily replaceable. When the person shows her selfishness and you have a fight, you should move away, move out, and move on, as the common thinking goes.

INTRODUCTION

And that thinking is reinforced by the reality that there are lots and lots of people to get re-involved with. My single friends are often unhappy with the quality of the person they are dating, but there seems to be no shortage of rebound relationships to pick from. You can find another job, you can find another church, and you can find new friends.

However, I must warn you of the very real danger of living in serial relationships. It is somewhat like a serial killer, in that with both cases there are bodies strewn all over the countryside and the person is hunting down another. It may be a relief to get rid of the bad one, but you haven't developed anything lasting. Life wasn't meant to be lived in several intense, short-term periods of relationships, at least the important relationships in life.

I remember a television interview many years ago in which a movie star with a reputation as a romancer was called by the host a "super lover," or something to that effect. The actor replied, "No, I'm not. The guy who has been happily married for fifty years is the super lover."

The fact that you're reading this book hopefully means you haven't decided to leave yet, if your button-pushing relationship is a severe one. You may be on your last try. You may be with a mild button-pusher and leaving isn't something you're considering. Or you may be in the middle, with a moderately crazy-making person that you're not sure you want to stay with.

Then there are those who, because of their circumstances, *can't realistically leave*. You may be in a job that you really need. You may have circumstances in your marriage that prohibit your leaving. There may be a family member who will remain in your life no matter what. If you are in this situation, I hope this book will change your *I can't leave* to an *I don't want to leave*. Many people over the years have learned how to help their button-pusher be an easier person to be around.

What, Me, a Button-Pusher?

OK, here's the bad news you need to look at: it is possible that you may be someone else's button-pusher! That isn't a fun thought to consider, but it is important. Remember, the nature of close relationships is that *we matter to each other, and we affect each other*. Without even knowing it, your attitudes and behaviors may be crazy-making for another person too.

You may be "guiltifying" your spouse or date when he says he doesn't want to go to a restaurant you like; for example: *After all I do for you, this is how you show your gratitude?* Or you may be attempting to control him in a covert way, such as, "I think maybe you really would like to visit my folks next weekend, wouldn't you?" It is helpful to be aware and open to this possibility, even that *you may be your button-pusher's button-pusher* in a mutually difficult dance. As the Bible teaches, "First take the plank out of your own eye, and then you will see clearly to remove the speck from your brother's eye" (Matthew 7:5).

You can't gauge if you are the button-pusher by the other's reaction to you, however. There are times when you may frustrate the other person, and that might be his problem, not yours. For example, saying no to verbal disrespect may cause the other person to say, "You are so oversensitive. I can't be myself around you; lighten up." That's certainly not a time to lighten up. Rather, it's a time to bear down and deal with the problem, as we will show you in this book. Make sure that what is yours is yours and what is his is his—an idea that we will develop later on.

Getting to the Changes

Having hope is not enough, however. Getting to the changes you want to see requires some elements and aspects of help. Following are what the principles in this book will provide for you as you prepare to deal effectively with your difficult person:

Understanding your button-pusher. Chapter 1 will discuss a broad picture of how button-pushers think, feel, and act in general. We will take a look at how the difficult person is hardwired underneath her childishness, control, disconnectedness, and so on. You will see what sort of things create a difficult person. Button-pushers view themselves, others, and the world in particular ways, and it helps to know about this.

Diagnosing the disease. Chapter 2 will provide tools to help you evaluate your own specific and particular situation. You need to know how to look at his behaviors, what might be causing them, and how severe the situation may be.

Understanding your own failed attempts. Many times you are confused because what would cause you to change (confrontation, reminders, entreaties) doesn't work for the button-pusher. Chapter 3 will help you get a picture of why this is so. This will help you give up what doesn't work and will never work, and get to what can work.

A vision for change. After chapter 4 you will have a clearer picture of what you want to see and experience in your button-pusher, both on the external level and inside also.

Providing the resources to navigate change. The bulk of your time will be spent here, in section 3 (chapters 6–11). You will learn the seven key resources that you have at your disposal that can be brought to bear upon your situation and relationship.

Resource #1: *God*—the one who promotes and empowers change

Resource #2: *Your Life*—all the ways you as a growing person can influence the relationship

Resource #3: *Others*—the powerful help that safe and sane people can bring

Resource #4: *Your Stance*—how you approach your button-pusher with your attitude and orientation to him and the problem

Resource #5: *Your Words*—what to say and how to say it

Resource #6: *Your Actions*—behaviors to execute that may be needed, such as consequences

Resource #7: *The Process*—knowing what to do over time, as time itself helps things change

You may find that your situation requires an overall approach with multifaceted interventions. Or it may be that a few ideas and concepts may shift things. Most people with a button-pusher find that it takes several resources and ideas that are integrated together, over time. But the advantage here is that you are in charge of the process, rather than the other person's issues running things. It just makes sense that *sanity should rule over insanity*. The path will give you the control to be an agent of change in the relationship.

Jump in, the Water's Fine

So start getting involved in this material. Be open to seeing things a new way. In fact, look at this as taking some steps of faith. Faith is about trusting in God's love and resources, even when they are not visible to our eyes. These principles originate in God's character, grace, and words.

Now let's take a look at why your button-pusher is the way he is and how he experiences the world.

PART ONE

Making Sense of
Your Crazymaker

THE VIEW FROM THE INSIDE:
HOW BUTTON-PUSHERS
ARE HARDWIRED

I WAS TALKING TO BRIAN AND CINDY, who were friends of mine, about their son Dylan. Dylan was in his mid-twenties and was a problem for them. He didn't finish college, had moved back home, wasn't keeping a steady job, had a chronically ungrateful attitude, and was showing indications of drug use. It was a real mess for them. The couple had tried to talk to Dylan, support him, encourage him to get a job and move out, and were habitually met with resentment, blame, and excuses.

They were telling me what they knew so that I'd understand enough to help them with some approach and strategies to improve things with Dylan. But while I was getting familiar with the circumstances, I noticed something else going on with Cindy. At first I didn't pay much attention to it, and it stayed on the periphery of my attention. But as the evening went on, it took more of center stage.

Cindy could not get past the fact that Dylan was not listening or responding to them. Over and over, in several different statements, she showed that she had not really accepted that he looked at life differently than she and Brian did. While Brian seemed to live in the reality more, Cindy was blown away and protesting what was really happening.

For example, she would say things to herself like, *I just cannot believe it. We've given him everything.* Or, *Why won't he listen and grow up?* Or, *We have tried to reason with him and give him support, but he acts like we're against him.*

All of these are pretty reasonable and natural responses when someone is causing difficulty in your life and isn't changing. But at some point you need to move past the shock and protest, accept things, and start taking actions. Cindy, however, was not ready for that.

I realized that nothing constructive would happen as long as Cindy stayed in her protest stage. She would continue to be surprised and astonished by what to me was a very common attitude among some young adults who refuse to take responsibility to grow up. And her surprise and astonishment would trip her up whenever Dylan showed her who he really was, and she would never be able to deal effectively with him.

So I used a metaphor that I have found very useful in similar situations. I said to Cindy, "Let me ask you a question. You're at the zoo. You're walking past the lion cage and you notice the door is wide open and the lion is coming out. He sees you. What do you think will happen next?"

Cindy went along with it: "I guess he would eat me."

"Probably so," I said. "And why would he do that?"

"Because he was hungry?"

"Sure, and for another reason: *it's what lions do.*"

Cindy's expression changed as the lights started turning on in her head: "So Dylan does this stuff because it's what he does?"

I said, "Well, yes, that's true. There are certainly more reasons than that. But the point is that Dylan is showing you that *who he is, is different from who you are*. You keep expecting a lion to listen to reason and walk back into the cage. That is what you would do; that's the rational thing to do. But that's not what lions do. They want to get out and hunt and feed."

I continued. "With Dylan, you keep thinking that he *should* get it, that he *should* see what a mess he's making of his life, that he *should* care about how he's affecting you guys. That's what you would do. And you seem to be constantly amazed that he doesn't listen to reason and keeps screwing up."

Brian said, "You know, honey, it's true. Every time we try to put a plan together, you cave in and get sort of paralyzed because you can't believe he'd be that selfish."

I added, "I bet that he can also work you over pretty good when he pretends to respond and get it, for a period of time. So you let up on him, and then he reverts."

Cindy said, "Story of my parenting life."

I said, "Certainly Dylan has problems, and is causing you lots of problems, and we will come up with some solutions. But nothing constructive will happen until you let go of your need for Dylan to be someone he isn't—at least he isn't today. You have to accept that he is different from the Dylan you want, that he is very different from you; he sees life in ways that you do not. And when you can do that, you can understand him and deal with who he really is in some good ways."

Cindy looked sad. I knew what was going on. Inside, she was beginning to enter a grief process. She was just starting to say good-bye to the Dylan she wanted her son to be, and to accept who he was, and that was a loss for her. But I also knew that, though painful, this would remove a major obstacle to helping Dylan change and grow.

GET THE PICTURE

You may be in Cindy's position, struggling to accept how in the world your button-pusher continues to do what he does. Or you may simply be baffled and confused by his ways. Either way, you do well to gain some understanding of how a difficult person is hard-wired underneath, so that you can be aware and prepared.

This might sound defensive, as if we are talking about preparing you for battle. In a way, you are in a war, the war to create an environment for growth and change with a person who has not shown signs of wanting that. But this is not a battle for power or possessions. It is a battle in which if you win, then he wins and the relationship wins. So it is a good thing to understand the psychology of the button-pusher.

THE PROBLEM IS NOT THE *Only* PROBLEM

This means getting beyond the troublesome behaviors and attitudes the person has. Behavior and attitude certainly can be a problem, but they are not *the* problem. They are manifestations, or symptoms, of the way he looks at life, and it is important to understand that. As Jesus said, "Every good tree bears good fruit, but a bad tree bears bad fruit" (Matthew 7:17). Look for the tree itself inside, rather than only dealing with the fruit.

As a psychologist, I see this happen all the time. The parent of an addict focuses only on detox (which is certainly often necessary) and not on internal change. The husband of a spendaholic wife wants to yank the credit cards without addressing why she spends indiscriminately. The woman whose boyfriend is two-timing her wants him to stop without dealing with why he is unfaithful. The person with a defensive co-worker on the job confronts him and tells him to stop avoiding taking responsibility. The result is that, all too often, when you end the symptom, the disease invades another part of the relationship. Whatever caused the fruit is still there, infecting things.

Alcoholics experts talk about a "dry drunk," for example: the alcoholic who stops drinking through willpower and discipline, with no self-scrutiny to figure out why he drank. Often, he will then become depressed or have anger problems that the drinking was medicating.

So don't get sidetracked by the behaviors, speech, or attitudes. Certainly you must deal with them, but get to what is really going on.

It Starts with the Insides

The best way to see this is to look at the basic architecture of people, that is, how they experience life, themselves, the world, and other people. This architecture is called *character*. The word has varied meanings, such as morality, honesty, and integrity, but actually it has a much broader understanding. Character is how you are made up inside, for good or for bad. It involves the values, feelings, and thoughts that you have, in patterns that help determine what you will do or say.

Elsewhere Dr. Henry Cloud and I have defined character as *that set of abilities you need to meet the demands of life*.[1] In other words, life places requirements on us all: to get along with people, to work well, to find our passion, and so forth. This applies not just to parenting but to all adult relationships as well. People need a certain combination of abilities called character which help them to pull off the many requirements of life.

There are six basic aspects to character. They can be summarized as the abilities to:

- Sustain meaningful relationships
- Take responsibility and have self-control in your life

- Live in the reality of your and others' imperfections
- Work and do tasks competently
- Have an internal moral structure
- Have a transcendent spiritual life

As you look at these and think about them, hopefully it is apparent that with these abilities, life goes pretty well. And the reverse is true: that many problems in life can be traced to deficits in these areas. You may have experienced that personally for yourself—in love, work, or your own habits and behaviors. The person who has difficulty being vulnerable has problems in intimacy. The individual who gives power away to others has no life and no self-control. The person who can't accept her imperfections struggles under shame and self-criticism, and so on.

We all have weaknesses and immaturities in at least one of these areas, to a greater or lesser level. Part of spiritual, emotional, and relational growth is to identify these and be in the healing and developing process.

THE HEART OF IT: AN OWNERSHIP PROBLEM

You, me, and our button-pushers are the same, in that we all have character issues. However, the most important aspect that sets the difficult person apart from other people, and that defines what a button-pusher truly is, is not that she has any of these deficits. Rather, it is that *she does not adequately own, or take responsibility for, her part in her issues*. In other words, she does not take sufficient agency for her weaknesses to change them and deal with how they affect other people.

Why is this so important? Because as most of us strive to shoulder our growth loads and learn to mature past them, the button-pusher remains stagnant in his immature state. He runs the risk of staying the same forever, or even getting worse, unless something external to him changes.

It is critical to understand this, so that you can deal with it. Anybody can have problems and weaknesses. That is what growing up and healing are all about. But the person who will not come to terms with his frailties, *especially with how they affect others*, has another problem and, literally, *is* a problem.

MY LIFE AS A BUTTON-PUSHER

OK, this next example is confession time. Here's an illustration of my own button-pushing. I have one of those sarcastic senses of humor which, while it can be fun for me and for my friends, can go too far and hurt someone. If a friend is late for lunch, I might say something like, "It's OK, I'm used to being treated by others this way." Now, with those I am close to, or with generally thick-skinned people, that sort of comment is not perceived as mean. But with someone who doesn't know me well, or has a sensitivity there, he may flinch inside and feel a bite.

For a long time, I didn't see any problems with that part of my humor; it was just kidding around. But my wife, Barbi, who is a gentler soul, started telling me that sometimes I hurt people's feelings. I figured she was being too sensitive and reading into people what wasn't there. But several years ago, I saw a guy I had known in high school who said, "I used to be terrified of being around you in a crowd." I asked why, and he said, "Because you would say something that would make me feel like a fool."

At that point, Barbi's remonstrations came back to me with the ring of truth, and I got it. I felt horrible and apologized to my friend, who was very gracious about it all. Over the years since then, I have worked pretty hard at making my jokes kinder with people. I'm not there yet, but from the feedback I've received, apparently a good deal of progress has been made in this area. I don't want to hurt anybody, and I didn't like knowing that I had.

But the point is this: before my high school friend confronted me, I was making life difficult for others and *not owning it*. Even in the face of Barbi's feedback, I wasn't taking responsibility for my bad behavior that affected others, and, at least in that area, I qualified as a button-pusher.

A Sad and Serious Case

A more severe example is a woman I knew who was so venomous that after her kids grew up and moved away, they wouldn't have anything to do with her. Her children were tremendously injured by her, and all struggled emotionally and relationally as a result.

I tried to get along with her as a friend, but you couldn't be with her a long time before she would launch into tirades about family members, friends, or whoever was available.

Before they gave up, her adult kids even had an intervention on her, where they gathered around in an intense meeting, to try to get through to her. They wanted a relationship with her and wanted their kids to know their grandmother. But she took all that as a personal attack and shunned them for a long time. Pastors and friends tried to make her aware of how destructive she was. She either went off on them or said they were trying to be mean to an old lady. She made herself impossible to reach. The last I heard of her, she was living in a little apartment by herself, with very little help, because she had run everyone off. In fact, on her refrigerator was a piece of paper with the handwritten words, *I'm not sorry.*

That is her life statement. That is it. And that symbolizes what I mean by a lack of ownership. What devastation she brought to her children and their children. What emptiness she brought on herself.

And what a contrast to what happens in heaven when someone says *I'm sorry* and repents! They have a party! "I tell you that . . . there will be more rejoicing in heaven over one sinner who repents than over ninety-nine righteous persons who do not need to repent" (Luke 15:7).

NOT REALLY BUTTON-PUSHERS

This is quite a different reality than a person who may have some serious relational difficulties but not a problem with ownership. That person can certainly push your buttons, but not in the same way. It is more that his issues and sins cause havoc, but it isn't because he doesn't care about them.

For example, a person I worked with in an organization was too critical and bossy of others. She was not a good listener, and I could see that it affected morale and productivity. Her control and harshness affected people in negative ways. It was pretty serious.

Yet when I began to talk to her about it, she melted and became very concerned. She truly didn't realize that she was doing this, and, once aware, she hated the reality that she did. She asked me and others for help, and to let her know when she was too bossy. She got into a spiritual growth group to get assistance and support. She read books on the subject. She prayed and read her Bible, searching for wisdom about her tendency.

It was a big problem, but she improved a great deal over time. The difference was that *she had a high sense of responsibility and ownership over her life, and she wanted to change in the right ways.* Certainly she pushed buttons, but her stance of ownership made all the difference. She didn't have to lose a job, or friends, or have a huge intervention, to change.

My friend isn't truly a button-pusher. She is motivated in her heart to change because she cares about others, and she cares about her growth. Those indeed are good motives for change. Einstein once said, "Man would indeed be in a poor way if he had to be restrained by fear of punishment and hope of reward after death." While these are certainly legitimate and valid motives, they are not all that are important. In the end, love is the highest motive, that is, love for God and for others: "As the Father has loved me, so have I loved you. Now remain in my love" (John 15:9).

WEAKNESS ISN'T BUTTON-PUSHING

I have another friend who has severe problems that affect her friends and family in negative ways. She suffers from a very long background of severe trauma, abuse, and neglect that most of us can't imagine. She has had financial, emotional, relational, and medical problems that have been profound, some of them related to her background, and some not. She has worked hard on this most of her life, diligently growing and changing. She has made major changes. But still her condition has been very troubling.

Thus, what she deals with affects those around her. Sometimes she will withdraw from life, and her support group will call her or visit her to keep her connected. Sometimes she has intense emotional outbursts, and those in her life must deal with them. Sometimes she has crises, and people who love her stay with her until it is resolved.

But she really isn't a button-pusher. She has worked harder in her personal growth than most people I know. She has given up more than most I know. She loves God in a very deep and personal way. She cares about her friends and hates it when she is a burden to them. She tries to help others with what resources she has.

I know one thing: her friends never resent her. They may feel drained by the demand that her problems bring to them, but they don't blame her. They never feel that she is taking advantage of their kindness, or that she isn't doing her part. In fact, sometimes they have to tell her, "Look, call us when you're in trouble. We don't like it when you shut us out."

And I know another thing: her struggles, by nature, are very, very different from her former ones. There are some people whose progress you cannot evaluate until you look at where they've come from. When you see where she has been, you marvel at the change.

That's not being a button-pusher. It is very different. That condition is what the Bible terms being *weak*, or broken in life. It is no sin to be weak. It is a problem that requires the resources, support, and love of us all. And it is a blessing and a privilege to partake in helping one of these individuals survive and grow: "Blessed is he who has regard for the weak; the LORD delivers him in times of trouble" (Psalm 41:1).

You may have a weak person in your life, and her weaknesses may push your buttons. Look at that as your problem, not hers, and deal with what that is about. Sometimes a weak person reminds us of our own frailties, and we react negatively to them. At other times, we overextend resources we don't have and feel exhausted by weak people, when we are the ones choosing to drain ourselves. This sort of thing is remedied by looking more at our issues than at theirs.

Think about the seasons of weakness you have experienced and how important it was to have warm, empathic people around you. I will never forget kindnesses people have done to me when I was depressed and in the dark nights of my soul. Their being there was truly a large part of my own healing and growth.

So focus on ownership. Whatever your button-pusher is doing that annoys or hurts you, it is secondary (unless you're in danger) to her failure to see her problem as a problem, and caring about it.

13

THE RULES ARE DIFFERENT

That brings further light on Cindy's confusion with her son Dylan. Cindy is the type of person who responds to normal confrontations and words. If someone tells her, "This bothers me," she takes it seriously, wants to not hurt someone else, and changes, sometimes to a fault.

Most of the time, the person in a relationship with a button-pusher is like that. That person (the "non-button-pusher") scrutinizes and evaluates how he himself is doing, listens to feedback, and tries to rectify situations, reconcile relationships, and become a better person. That is a good thing. If you have to be off-balance in one direction or another, it is better to care about others' feelings a little too much than not enough.

The button-pusher has different rules. Soul-searching, confrontation, feedback, and another person's hurt feelings don't really affect him to change. He rationalizes, denies, minimizes the difficulty he causes, or blames the other person. So be aware that what works for you may not work for him.

LOOKING AT YOU AND THE WORLD

You also need a glimpse of how a button-pusher sees life and relationships, because it most likely is not how you do. Most people, with variations, see that their lives and feelings matter, but so do others'. They feel bad inside if their immaturity, irresponsibility, or selfishness bothers someone. That is empathy. They look at their bad stuff and deal with it.

The button-pusher often sees themselves as more central to things. Their experience tends to be the more important one, and that is why it is difficult to problem-solve with them. Sometimes they become angry. Sometimes they may think they are a persecuted victim. They often have a diminished capacity to have empathy for the feelings of others, *especially for how they hurt others*. And it is very difficult for them to take a long and hard look at their own darkness, admit it, and deal with it.

So if you are in an argument with your button-pusher, which is generally a waste of time, and you find yourself thinking, *We aren't talking from the same place,* you are likely right. If you are trying to be loving, honest, and owning, and yet things aren't working out, it may be that your button-pusher is perceiving you as nagging, blaming, persecutory, controlling, or, worst of all, insignificant. Though this may be painful, it is very instructive to know so that you can deal with it in the latter part of this book.

It hurts to be vulnerable to another person and receive little empathy from them. But realize that is one part of the problem, and deal with those feelings with people who do have something to offer you, especially as you get ready to approach this person with the idea of change.

COMFORTABLE IN THE DYSFUNCTION

Often, the button-pusher has been that way for a long time. Therefore, she experiences little discomfort in how she is. She is used to controlling and manipulating others. Or she can cut herself off and punish people with long periods of silence. Or she has no problem spending all the money because she is sure there will always be more.

The mark of a growing person is that, though he accepts where he is, by God's help he is not going to stay where he is. He wants to heal, grow, and change, for his sake, for God's sake, and for the sake of those around him. He is not content to exist in his current state of immaturity. That is why one of the agendas of this book is to help you help the button-pusher be less comfortable in his dysfunction, so that he will want things to change.

The Good with the Bad

In researching this book, I encountered a lot of material that really bashed difficult people, as if they are totally bad, evil, or sick. While there certainly are some really bad, evil, and sick people out there, the reality is that your button-pusher probably has some very good aspects to himself that you need to keep in perspective. This might be warmth, a sense of humor, good structure, popularity with people, and many other things.

Don't negate these, for then you aren't relating to your button-pusher as he really is, and he is likely to feel judged and condemned by you. As this book will develop, you want to be strict on the issues, but warm toward the person. That's how all of us want to be treated, and that is what works best.

Why Doesn't My Button-Pusher "Own His Stuff"?

This is important to understand, because it will help dictate your approach to him when we get to that part of the book. People don't take responsibility for more than one reason. Here are some of the more important ones.

Lack of Knowledge and Experience

Sometimes it is simply a matter of not knowing and not understanding the world of relationships, emotions, growth, and spirituality—what most would call the inner world, or the deeper life. Your button-pusher's life experience may have been bereft of those processes. He may have grown up in a loving, hardworking family that never talked about these matters. Or he may have had a lot of chaos in his life, so he turned away from the inside in order to manage people and circumstances by staying busy.

There is little awareness of emotional realities in this situation. When you say, *You're too direct with me, and it hurts my feelings*, he may think you're speaking an alien language. He literally doesn't know what these words mean. He's just trying to tell you the truth about something, and it doesn't hurt his feelings when people are very direct. He isn't fighting you; he just doesn't know this world. This person often responds well to getting in some structured safe setting, such as a growth group, where he can begin to open himself up to the intangibles of life and relationship.

Fear

Some difficult people will resist hearing feedback or looking at their ways because they are afraid. They may have a fear of being seen as a really bad person. Sometimes they will truly feel that they are, in reality, a really bad person. Or that others will not like them, or will leave them. Still others have a fear, deep within, that if they become aware of what they are doing, they will be overwhelmed by it and suffer some sort of breakdown.

I once counseled a man who tended to run people off with his brusqueness and coldness. He had ruined a couple of marriages, alienated his kids, and had large business problems. On the surface, he seemed to not care about all that and shrugged it all off. When people would tell him how off-putting he was, he would say, *That's their problem*. On the surface, he sounded like a truly selfish button-pusher.

But that was not this man's entire script. As he started feeling safer in the counseling, something inside him began to change and shift. He began to feel his neediness, loneliness, and dependency. He experienced the condition that we all have, the need for relationship. Along with that awareness came another awareness, that of a deep terror. He became afraid he would be so vulnerable to others that people would be able to really hurt him.

It was ironic, because that's what happened anyway. He pushed people away because he was afraid that people would leave him, and thus the stage was set for what he most feared to happen.

What occurred instead was that he faced the demons inside, allowed himself to reach out for help and comfort from some good, safe people, and the opposite happened. He was met at the point of his need, and he experienced the grace and warmth that he had always wanted but had never trusted.

Guess what? His crusty outer shell began to dissolve, and over time, he gradually became more emotionally responsive, tender, and empathic. The fear-based button-pusher has a lot of hope, if he is willing to look at what is underneath.[2]

Entitlement and Self-Centeredness

Entitlement and self-centeredness refer to the tendency to look at life as a privileged person. The individual believes, secretly or overtly, that he is special and above others. He should not be subjected to the same rules that others must be. In a matter of speaking, he shouldn't have to wait in line for his football tickets.

Often, the entitled person is self-absorbed, grandiose, and has little awareness of the feelings of others. For him, others exist dimly, and only as objects that meet his interests at the time. He gets along with them when they fulfill his needs, but not when they exercise freedom or difference.

Sometimes these individuals come from backgrounds in which they were not given limits and realistic self-perceptions by their significant relationships. The grandiosity comes from no one lovingly popping the balloon of selfishness to help them see that others are as important and special as they are.

I was working with Rich and Margaret, a married couple. Margaret was the entitled button-pusher. Her self-centeredness was wrecking their marriage. I tried a well-known communication and empathy exercise with them to further diagnose the problems. I said, "I want each of you to tell the other one thing that bothers you about him or her. Then I want the other person to paraphrase it, trying it enough times until the spouse says, 'Yes, you understand what I am saying that bothers me about you.'"

Margaret went first. She said, "You don't say anything about what's wrong, then you get too angry at me and the kids. That really frustrates and scares me."

I looked at Rich, and he said, "OK, I think you're saying that I withdraw and then blow up, and that makes you angry and frightens you, and you would like me to stop."

I looked at Margaret, and she agreed that he had pretty much gotten it.

Rich's turn. He said, "When I confront you on a problem, even in a nice way, you either rationalize it or get mad at me, and I feel all by myself in the marriage."

I looked at Margaret. She said, "Well, I do that because you're so negative."

I said, "Stop there. That wasn't paraphrasing; it was a reaction. Try it again."

Margaret said, "You're blowing things out of proportion."

"Tilt," I said. "You're telling Rich your thoughts, not hearing his. Try again."

This time she was mad at Rich and me both. She said hotly, "All you guys care about is putting me on the spot."

I said, "That's not all I care about, but it points out where we need to pay attention. You're not going to get any of the good things you want in this marriage, Margaret, until you begin to care about Rich's feelings and experience as much as you care about yours." And that is where we began concentrating the work.

The entitled button-pusher often reacts negatively to feedback and confrontation. It is offensive, and an affront to his elevated self-perception. Confrontation injures the view of how he has constructed himself. He tends to react to the truth in anger or withdrawal, "shooting the messenger."

This is sad, because the truth could likely save the entitled person. To learn and experience how lonely his selfishness is making him, and how he is not in reality what he thinks he is, would help him become aware of the emptiness within his shell. Then he could be filled up, rebuilt, and transformed by the love and truth of God and safe people. And I have seen it happen many times. There is a lot of hope for the entitled button-pusher, with the right approach.

Envy

Envy is one of the darkest products of Adam and Eve's fall from grace in the garden of Eden. It guarantees misery to the person, and to those he loves. Envy is *the demand that what will make me happy is what I do not possess*. It keeps you empty, hungering, resenting others who have good relationships and circumstances, and lusting for more.

Envy is not desire. Desire can be a very good thing, for it drives us to get what we need: goals, jobs, people we want in our lives, opportunities, and the like. And when the desire is fulfilled, the person experiences peace and contentment.

The opposite is true with envious people. When they get the promotion, the money, the relationship, or whatever, it is not enough. Something else, outside of them, replaces it as the reason they're not happy. In fact, they often are not happy until someone else is unhappy. Then they feel some sense of justice in the world.

The envious button-pusher is terminally unhappy as a result but does not see that as his problem. The problem is seen as the wife who doesn't support him enough; the boss who demands too much;

the economy that is wrecked; the church that doesn't meet his needs; the children who aren't following as they should. And the result is that people around him feel that insatiability. They may try to appease it, but it is never good enough. The envy takes the love, support, and kindness and renders it impotent and unimportant.

The resolution of our envy problems will always center on experiencing their result—which is spiritual, relational, and emotional poverty—and on learning gratitude. Gratitude is being thankful for the good gifts, people, and things we do have. Gratitude puts us in the position of the old saying: Happiness isn't having what you want, but wanting what you have.

Emotional Conditions

Sometimes a person will have an emotional or psychological disorder which renders her less able to see what she is doing. Some acute depressions, for example, make it difficult for a person to see beyond her pain, to see the effect she has on others. Anxiety, panic, and addictive processes can also distort the thinking of the button-pusher. This does not mean she wants to stay stuck in whatever she is doing. Rather, she is stuck in a pain syndrome that is clouding her thinking and functioning in the world. This person may respond well to counseling to clear these matters up.

Sin and Evil

Keep in mind that all of us have tendencies to go our own way, away from God's care and his path. We miss the mark. That is the essence of sin and evil. It comes in many forms, including some of the causes of ownership problems listed above, and in a large range of severity. Some individuals are acutely aware of their own internal darkness, and dedicate themselves to confessing and bringing their tendencies to the light of God and his people. Others have a shallow view of their sin, or do not see it when it is there. And others have given themselves over to the control of sin.

Your button-pusher may have a blindness about himself, or even a rebellion against God. That sort of spiritual stance can cause a person to miss seeing what is inside that needs to be healed by grace and the power of God. Repentance and turning toward God may be needed in a direct manner here.

Supernatural Causes

There is a real devil, whose agenda is to devour lives and remove people from God's care: "Be self-controlled and alert. Your enemy the devil prowls around like a roaring lion looking for someone to devour" (1 Peter 5:8). I have witnessed the supernatural force of demonic influence and believe it is actual, just as it is taught in the Bible. Since one of Satan's strategies is to tempt people away from God, it makes sense that there are times that a button-pusher's lack of responsibility, attitude of blame, or denial could have a demonic origin.

At the same time, the Bible teaches a balance of factors. Not every problem has a demon under a rock. But some do. If you suspect this sort of force at work, find people in your spiritual community who have expertise and experience in these matters, and who also believe in the power of emotional, psychological, and medical issues.

Psychiatric or Medical Issues

There also are times in which a person's medical or psychiatric condition distorts their perceptions of reality. This can also influence how clearly they may be aware of their issues. For example, thought disorders, psychotic processes, hallucinations, and the like can wreak havoc on a person's ability to understand what is going on. It is always good to consult with a psychiatrist if you suspect there is evidence of a disorder.

Whatever factor or combination of factors has influenced your button-pusher to be the way he is, keep a balance in mind. Certainly he is responsible for the crazy-making things he does to you, and he needs to change those. But at the same time, quite likely there were injuries done to him via significant relationships that caused a bent in him in that direction too. Button-pushers are, as is the case with all of us, both dispensers and recipients of trouble in life. Keep the balance.

Also, whatever the cause or causes, use the resources in section 3 to help move the person to addressing them. You may want him or her to admit a problem, change a behavior, restrain an attitude, get into a growth context, or seek other help. The resources are to equip you to help your button-pusher take whatever next step is necessary.

REALITY IS LARGER THAN WE ARE

Here is some encouragement as you get to understand your button-pusher: *his lack of ownership should create problems for him.* That's not being mean; it is just true, and it means hope for you and for him.

Reality is larger than we are. As I mentioned in the introduction, God has designed us so that if we live according to his ways, life works pretty well. But if we don't, life begins to fall apart. You don't fight long against gravity, magnetism, or nuclear force. The big realities always win. We should reap what we sow, in the good or bad consequences of our lives.

So the button-pusher's lack of awareness and resistance to taking responsibility should cause life not to work well for him. And that can be a great incentive to change. For example, a man with a hot temper who won't listen *should* encounter relationship and job problems. A mother who is invasive and intrusive and won't listen *should* annoy people in her life, who will then avoid her or not be real with her. An irresponsible adult child who won't listen *should*, at some point, have to live on his own and find a job, even though his quality of life isn't what he is used to.

These factors aren't punitive, any more than getting drenched from standing in the rain is punitive. It's just how reality works, and those who bend their knee to God's reality principles tend to do better than those who do not.

But suppose you are thinking, *OK, my button-pusher isn't having problems or suffering any consequences. He's doing fine. He's happy. I'm the one who's miserable.* I have heard that question in so many forms over the years. And the million-dollar question I want you to wonder about is this: *Are you helping your button-pusher to avoid experiencing the problems he needs to experience?*

Think about ways that you might be enabling or rescuing your button-pusher from experiencing his own life problems. Maybe you're always there for him, or threaten without following through, or encourage without confronting. It is worthwhile—and one of the things we will get to—to analyze if you are part of the problem. If you find that you are, that is very good news. The person who is concerned can now make some choices to make the situation different.

DIAGNOSING THE DISEASE:
UNDERSTANDING YOUR SPECIFIC
SITUATION

NOW IT'S TIME TO MOVE from button-pushing in the main to your own particular situation. The more clarity you can have about your button-pusher's specific tendencies, the better you will be able to use our seven resources to bear upon the situation. (You'll find them in chapters 5–11.)

Taking such a close and personal look may be harder than it seems. It is very easy for our emotions, memories, frustrations, and the general life damage that the relationship brings to the front of our minds to cloud our thoughts. But until you can realistically and carefully "diagnose the disease" metaphorically speaking, you will find yourself reacting, being pulled this way and that, feeling helpless and impotent, and without any sort of meaningful and structured path to follow.

So for this chapter, get some distance, either emotionally or physically. Get with a friend, go to the library, stay late at work, or check into a hotel if you have to, so that your mind can objectively figure out your situation. Here are the things to look at.

WHAT PROBLEM DOES MY BUTTON-PUSHER CAUSE?

Determine what things affect your life and the relationship itself as a result of your button-pusher's actions or attitudes. Remember that any relationship involves certain mutual needs, requirements, and expectations. Things like love, respect, and responsibility should be happening in a good, meaningful flow between you two for the relationship to be functioning well. What are the specific things that are interrupting that flow? Here are some examples.

- My boyfriend drinks too much.

- My ex-wife makes custody issues a nightmare.

- My husband is withdrawn and distant.

- My wife sees every problem as my fault and blames me.

- Nothing I do is good enough for my boss.

- A co-worker is spreading lies about me.

- My husband is putting us in financial jeopardy.

- I can't depend on my co-worker to carry his load.

- My dad scares me with his temper.

- My teenaged daughter is out of control.

- My wife spends too much.

- My husband is into Internet porn.

- My mom calls and visits too much.

- My girlfriend alternates between clinginess and anger with me.

- My friend is indirect about the truth.

- My partner can't have a discussion without cutting me off.

- I can't depend on my friend to be reliable and responsible.

- My adult child is on drugs, or won't get a job and leave home.

As you can see from this brief list, sometimes the button-pusher causes a life problem such as being the alcoholic in the family, or financial risk, or infidelity. At other times, it is a relationship problem such as loss of trust, safety, and love. And it can be both. But it is important to clearly state what disruption in life is going on. Otherwise, things can become so broad and general that nothing can be done. Saying *He can be such a jerk* or *She's impossible* are statements made in frustration, but aren't helpful in focusing on what is going on.

This isn't to say that your button-pusher isn't causing lots of different problems, which makes it harder to focus on one thing. You may have a person in your life who is moody, irresponsible, and a substance abuser all at the same time. This is not uncommon at all. If that is the case, identify all of them. The important thing here, however, is not to determine everything that bothers you, but *everything significant that is a problem*. A rageaholic who doesn't pick up his socks should probably have to first deal with the anger rather than the sloppiness. Stay with the main, big-picture actions or attitudes that put you in jeopardy, are ruining the relationship, keep you up at night, and generally permeate your life in a negative way. This is a war, though hopefully it is a war of love. So pick the battles that matter the most.

How Severe Is the Matter?

There are different levels of seriousness in a problem. This is important for you, as it will help determine your course of action. If is not very severe, just troubling, you have time to thoughtfully plan out your approach. This also means that you probably will not need an army of resources and experts to help you. Perhaps the person scares you with his temper, but you only experience it a few times a year.

If it is moderately severe, you will need to spend more time, energy, and resources. For example, the person's temper tantrum might occur often in fits of rage and disrupts family functioning.

If it is extremely severe and urgent, however, there may be physical violence. At this level, someone could be in danger and you may need to take quick action; for example, calling someone for help, finding a shelter, or even calling the police.

The point here is for you to understand the range of your problem clearly. Scrutinize yourself about this too. I know some people who see every relational misdemeanor as a felony, and they drive friends away. They treat someone who is five minutes late the same way as they treat someone who breaks into convenience stores. Be honest about severity: mildly irritating, causing intimacy and love disruptions, creating family chaos, or causing damage or danger. This will help you to be ready for your action steps.

GOING DEEPER: WHAT DRIVES THE BUTTON-PUSHING?

This requires a little more digging. As I have mentioned earlier, there are underlying character and personal traits that tend to influence a person to be a crazy-maker. The life problem is generally a fruit of deeper matters. This isn't to say that she is not responsible for her behaviors and the trouble she causes. She is totally responsible, as we all are: "All have sinned" (Romans 3:23).

However, *total responsibility does not equate to total ability*. Just because the addicted adult child is responsible for using drugs doesn't mean he has the power or wherewithal to become clean and sober. Just because the husband into porn is responsible for stopping doesn't mean he has the capacity to stop. There are strong and dark forces moving in all of us, including believers in Christ, and we still need grace, love, support, truth, wisdom, and time to mature into people who can change over time.

That is a tough message of the Bible: We are responsible, but we cannot transform ourselves. This forces us to look outside of our own strength to God and his answers to solve that dilemma.

Your button-pusher may not seem to be struggling to stop, or even recognize that she has a problem. So she is even further from God's solution, as people who blind themselves do not seek him to open their eyes. But whether or not your difficult person knows or admits he needs to change, he does. And yet he cannot truly transform without help and grace.

Having said all that, you do need to look further than the behavior your button-pusher is doing. You need to ask him to change more than the behavior. Otherwise, you run the risk of seeing it again and again and again, sometimes in different forms. Focus on the root, not just the fruit.

Possible Causes or Influences

To flesh this out, let's look again at our list of problems. This time, let's examine the possible causes or influences. I have listed a couple for each problem. One tends to be somewhat generous; the other is a little more serious. Your person could have elements of both, and there could be many more possible causes for each life problem.

This is just a way to get your analytic juices flowing so that you can be looking at the patterns of the problems, and what leads to them. In some cases, if you find that you are overwhelmed or confused by the complexity of your button-pusher, seek out a counselor or therapist and tell her what you know, asking for clarification. These sorts of meetings and consults can be very illuminating in focusing on what is really going on.

Life Problem	Possible Causes
My boyfriend drinks too much	• He hasn't become an adult yet • He is medicating internal pain
My ex-wife makes custody issues a nightmare	• She wants to punish • She is obsessive and overly concerned
My husband is withdrawn and distant	• He is unable to open up emotionally • He is self-absorbed
My wife sees every problem as my fault and blames	• She feels powerless and projects blame • She refuses to look at her own contributions
Nothing I do is good enough for my boss	• He is critical • He is isolated from relationship in his life
A co-worker is spreading lies about me	• She does not confront people directly • She sees people as black and white
My husband is putting us in financial jeopardy	• He is impulsive and has little self-control • He lacks empathy for the distress he causes
I can't depend on my co-worker to carry his load	• He is irresponsible and not diligent • He is overwhelmed and says "yes" too much
My dad scares me with his temper	• He intimidates when he needs to admit he is wrong • He avoids feeling helpless when he can't control someone

My teenaged daughter is out of control	• She doesn't have, or refuses, structure and authority • She is disconnected and isolated
My wife spends too much	• She is immature • She is meeting some need in a symbolic way
My husband is into Internet porn	• He retreats to fantasy to avoid some negative reality • He feels helpless and powerless around his wife
My mom calls and visits too much	• She is dependent and has not developed a support system • She is intrusive and has few boundaries
My girlfriend alternates between clinginess and anger with me	• She is dependent and has not developed a support system • She is intrusive and has few boundaries
My friend is indirect about the truth	• He is afraid of the conflict that comes with honesty • He prefers things to be easy than honest
My partner can't have a discussion without cutting me off	• He does not tolerate different opinions well • He feels hated when he is disagreed with
I can't depend on my friend to be reliable and responsible	• She relies on good intentions rather than faithfulness • She overcommits too much
My adult child is on drugs, or won't get a job and leave home	• He feels no concern about taking care of his own life • He does not possess the skills to enter life

DON'T BE THE SHRINK

This information isn't about overwhelming you with data so you can fix or rescue your difficult person. Don't think you have to figure out everything there is to know about the person's family of origin issues, his internal world, his sin patterns, his brokenness, or his issues. You just need to know broad brush strokes that are true, real, and validated by experience and other safe and sane people so that you can know better what your responses are to be. Don't get stuck in the paralysis of analysis.

SEVERITY AT THIS DEEPER LEVEL

Earlier, we looked at how severe the life problem of the button-pusher is. Now do the same here, but in a different way. While the "fruit" level of severity revolved around how the problems affect life, from bothersome to truly dangerous, this is not the same. At the "cause" level, what you need is to be able to understand how deeply the character issues listed above go inside the person. This will also help you to prepare and resource yourself for your approach.

For example, is the emotional distance of your husband so profound that he speaks to no one in his life about anything but news and sports? Or can he talk about personal issues at some level but not deeply? Or does he open up with others but not with you specifically? This is important information.

Here's another example. Is your adult child's lack of taking responsibility for her life so problematic that she never makes any moves to become independent of you and feels entitled to your caretaking? Or does she move out and fail and move back in, hating it all the time? Or does she ask you for money when she should be providing her own?

For a third example of severity, take the critical person. Does she incessantly find fault for large and small, real and perceived offenses, with no sense of what she does? Or is she out of balance, between praise and criticism? Or is she OK with others but just comes down on you?

Thinking through the severity issues will also help you be prepared to marshal the necessary resources to address the problem of your button-pusher.

TAKE THE TEMPERATURE OF THE OWNERSHIP PROBLEM

This is your home base—the beginning of everything, as we noted in chapter 1. Your button-pusher most likely avoids taking ownership, or responsibility, for both the life/relationship problem and for the underlying dynamics influencing him. Perhaps he doesn't see it, or is afraid to, or thinks it's all you, or it's not as bad as you think. Whatever the nature of the ownership, it is important for you to understand it. This is because, ultimately, *the solution resides in the responsibility of the problem resting on the button-pusher's shoulders, not someone else's.*

So how severe is your person's lack of ownership? Is it minimal, that is, is she the kind of person that just needs an empathic but clear confrontation to become aware of her problem and shake her out of her tree a little? Is it more serious than that, such as someone who sees what she does but excuses it, rationalizes it, or minimizes how bad it is? Or is it worse, where, even if she knows she does it, she blames it on you or others (*If it weren't for you . . .*)?

Does she deny at all that she even does the things she does? That is, some people will deny an objective reality that has been witnessed by other people. Then sometimes people will weave in and out of denial, which makes understanding it more complicated. When they feel safe and loved, they will admit they are difficult, but when they are afraid or threatened, they will deny it.

One of the most difficult levels of ownership is the person who

WHO'S PUSHING YOUR BUTTONS?

does admit she does something problematic but simply doesn't care. That is, she owns the behavior or attitude but has a lack of concern for its effect on other people. When you become aware of this, it conveys a level of seriousness, for an empathic failure must be addressed, usually using consequences and limits, before there can be any problem solving.

I once dealt with a friend who was going to leave his wife for another woman, destroying the family. I had clearly told him what he was doing to himself, his wife, and his kids over a fantasy. He told me he understood that, but he was going ahead with the divorce. I then said, "I just want you to know that in a case like this, you will also most likely lose a great deal of contact with your kids, not to mention the court's ruling on your finances. And if I am asked about it, I will side against you. I don't want to do that, but the reality is that you are consciously choosing a path that is hurting several people, and you are only thinking of yourself."

He was really angry at me for supposedly betraying him. But fortunately he talked to some other people who also told him that he was headed for disaster. It wasn't empathy for his family that helped him turn around. It was the prospect of losing his kids and his money, a much lower motive. But the concern about these losses did slow down what he was planning long enough for him to get into the process of growth. It was not a fast track of growth. His wife took a long time to heal, and longer to trust. He eventually worked through the issues, and they reconnected at a much better and deeper level, ultimately moving on with their marriage intact.

CAN'T VERSUS WON'T

This is an important aspect to look at as you figure out what is going on with your difficult person. Is she unable (*can't*), or is she resistant (*won't*), or is she some combination of both? Obviously, the more inability you see, and the less resistance you see, the better off things are. God provides all sorts of help and support for the "can'ts" of this world, as they know they are broken and need him to put them together. They are like a broken arm that requires safety and a splint. But the "won'ts" often need to experience the consequences of their stubbornness to finally wave the white flag of surrender and admit that they truly "can't." They are less like a broken arm than a lazy muscle that doesn't want to be exercised!

How do you determine this? For one thing, look at the level of concern the person has for what he does. Does he feel true and authentic remorse for the pain and difficulty he causes by his issues? If so, he may not even be a real button-pusher, but simply a struggling and weak person. Is his life marked by a general sense of care for others, and responsibility for himself? That argues for inability. Or does he manifest a deficit of empathy and a failure to take ownership of what he does? That speaks for resistance.

There also is a more covert but fairly common form of this problem you need to be aware. It is resistance *disguised* as inability, or a *won't* posing as a *can't*. Here the button-pusher is aware enough that he understands that he will get kinder treatment if he appears broken and yet trying, and perhaps people will rescue him. So he presents himself in a wounded light, rather than a rebellious one.

For example, I had a person in group counseling who would be critical of other people, and not in a loving way. Then she would laugh and say, "JK" (just kidding). When people in the group confronted her on it, she would sort of collapse into tears, saying, "I didn't mean it, it's my past coming to haunt me." Then the people she had just attacked would try to comfort her, instead of her being sorry and comforting them. I let this go on a few rounds, just to make sure about it, because at first I thought she just needed a chance to get things out in the open. But the behavior continued, and people were getting hurt.

So I said to her one night, "Amy, I'm sorry, but while I do believe you're a sensitive person, I just don't think you're as fragile as you appear, nor as sorry as you appear. It seems that you are using this issue to be able to be angry at people without having to then experience their anger at what you do. That's not fair, nor is it good for you or them."

Needless to say, Amy was very upset at my statement and wanted to leave. But the group supported her and told her they really cared, while at the same time they affirmed that they thought she was more resistant than broken in that area. To her credit, Amy was able to see that she had spent her life being afraid to be direct with others, so she always took pot shots when she was angry, instead of confronting face to face. She began to learn what she was afraid of, and how to safely be an honest person. In time, she did very well in her work.

The point is, go for what you and other safe people see, not just what your button-pusher says. Doing shows more than saying. God designed us to be honest, and if people aren't, something should disconnect inside you, saying, *Watch out*. Pay attention to covert signals.

A Process Rather Than an Event

The exercise of diagnosing the disease will involve time and energy. *Do not rush this*. In fact, it is probably best to do this sort of work over several time periods so that you can reflect and meditate on what is really going on. Don't overstate or understate the nature and severity of the button-pusher's condition. That is why it is important that you be well into the process of doing your own work, as we will go over in the next chapter, to keep your eye clear and undistorted by your own pain, reactions, and perceptions.

In this way, you will be able to more effectively take the steps to help your person change and grow.

PART TWO

Leaving Your Past to Create Your Future

CLEAR THE DECK:
UNDERSTANDING YOUR FAILED ATTEMPTS

O<small>K, KAREN</small>," I said to my friend, "I agree. If everything you have told me is true, your father is pretty much out there, and he is doing some bad stuff."

Karen, who was in her mid-thirties, had just told me some more stories about her dad, who I had never met but who sounded like a nightmare button-pusher. Over the years of our friendship, she had let me know some of the destructive things he had been and done. He was mean and belittling to her mom. He criticized Karen unmercifully when they talked. He was combative in social gatherings and embarrassed her, or he got quiet and sulked for days when things didn't go his way. He was a generally negative person to anyone in his family. Karen had wanted to talk to me about the difficulty of having such a dad, a thought I agreed with her on.

She said, "How should I deal with him?"

I said, "Well, how much are you contributing to the problem?"

That question seemed to bug her. "What do you mean?" she said. "I'm not the problem. He is."

"I understand he seems really, really difficult. He sounds awful. But I'm asking what your part is."

"What is my part? What are you talking about? I'm the one who's subjected to verbal abuse. I'm the one who has to call him on the phone to make up. I'm the one who has to put Mom back together after he rants all over her and hurts her feelings. He made my childhood a walking hell. Are you saying I'm like him?"

"No, no, no," I protested. "From what you have told me, he takes no responsibility for his hurtfulness, and I know that you are not that kind of person at all, so let's don't even go there. But I can tell you that from what you've told me over the years, there are some things you've done that have made things worse."

"What sort of things?" She was pretty guarded, and I couldn't blame her. But she was the one who had asked me for advice, and I didn't want to see her button-pusher dad keep ruining things for her, so I went for it.

"Well, OK, you appease him when he is critical, so that he feels no discomfort. He is cruel, and then you call and apologize for setting him off. You get all hopeful and happy on his good days, and think it is a sign that he is changing, when he's just resting up to have the energy to be mean the next day. Then you aren't prepared and ready when he blasts again. You avoid directly confronting him, as does everyone, so he never gets accurate feedback on what he is doing. You don't insist that he get any sort of counseling or help, because it might set him off. Your mom is isolated and weak, and you don't push her to get in some supportive group or church or something so that she can stand up to him. When your brother and sister are mad at him, you step in and mediate so that he doesn't have to be upset.

"Karen, your dad sounds like a very difficult man, and that is largely his choice and responsibility. But I want you to be aware that there are things you are doing that are helping to keep him sick and mean, and you can do something about them. They are *your* baggage, and I would be glad to take a look at them with you, if that would help."

Although it wasn't fun, Karen was responsive to what I was saying. She paid attention. I was proud of her. She wasn't crazy about what I had said—who would have been? But after we talked, she did go and take some of these steps I mentioned, and things did begin to improve.

DON'T BE PART OF THE PROBLEM

My conversation with Karen illustrates a principle: *To the extent you avoid owning your part in the problem, you will continue in the problem.*

If your approach, attitude, or behavior to the button-pusher isn't healthy, you must deal with it and change it. If there is an aspect in your relationship with your button-pusher in which you are making a contribution, you will hamper any growth and change by not attending to it. In other words, if you see yourself as 100 percent innocent, and your button-pusher as 100 percent at fault in every aspect of the issue, you are paralyzing yourself from changing things.

Now you may be having a Karen-type reaction to this idea and tensing up defensively a little, but hang tight and it will begin to make sense. As we saw with Karen, which we will go into more later, there are things that you either do or avoid doing that help the button-pusher not change and grow.

Having said that, there are absolutely many, many situations in which the person bears no fault with the button-pusher. These might include unprovoked criticism, irresponsibility, abuse, trauma, assault, and the like. These sorts of horrible things become matters of protection, healing, and forgiveness. But in many other aspects of a difficult relationship, you can have some control, freedom, and choice if you are aware of what you might be doing that is not helping matters.

To clarify this, nobody is perfect—we all sin and miss the mark. That's why all of us need a Savior. At the same time, there are different levels of immaturity, hurtfulness, and evil. Some people say that each person in a relationship contributes fifty-fifty to the problems. I don't believe that is true at all. Jesus even said that some matters are weightier than others.[1]

So your contribution, like Karen's, may be much less weighty than your button-pusher's contribution. You may have less baggage than the difficult person. You may be more legitimately in the right about what is going on. At the same time, that does not let you off the hook to do your own cleanup work and look at ineffective ways you are handling the relationship.

Jesus had a pretty direct statement about this: "You hypocrite, first take the plank out of your own eye, and then you will see clearly to remove the speck from your brother's eye" (Matthew 7:5).

Whether you are aware of it or not, *you already have adopted ways of dealing, surviving, or trying to fix your button-pusher.* They may not be formalized or written down, but you have crafted them. And you are probably not happy with their results either. So it's time to let them go. It is very valuable to unearth what is not working so that you can clear your own deck and make room in your head and in your life for what can work.

We need to look at some of the primary unsuccessful things we do with button-pushers, why we do them, and how we can *stop doing them.*

However, before you begin, the first thing you will need to do, and it is very important to do this soon, is to ask a difficult question of yourself: *Is this situation real, is it just my perception, or is it both?*

Is It You or the Other?

You need to investigate and sort out thoroughly what is true, accurate, and real in your relationship with your button-pusher, and what is based on your own feelings, distortions, old baggage, and expectations.

Just because you have negative feelings about a person doesn't mean he has done anything wrong, or has been as wrong as you observe him to be. He may be doing little things that you perceive are huge things.

For example, a man with an aging father may go to visit him. The father may be somewhat irritable or demanding with him. To most people, that might be annoying or bothersome, but that's about the extent of it. Yet to the adult son, it may take him back to an unresolved and unredeemed past when he was a little boy with that father, and the bad attitude cut more deeply into him at that age. He may then respond as if the attitude were re-wounding the original injury, because he has not healed. So he may think that his father is impossible, hugely destructive and out of control, when actually he is just a cranky old man.

This is where activities such as asking God for clarity on the situation (chapter 5), doing your own growth and healing (chapter 6), and getting feedback from others (chapter 7) will be invaluable to help you discern what is real and how severe your button-pusher's condition truly is. When the facts are not clear, it is better to consider someone innocent until proven guilty. That is the law of mercy, which we all want applied to us as well: "For judgment will be merciless to one who has shown no mercy; mercy triumphs over judgment" (James 2:13 NASB).

How would you like it if someone considered you their button-pusher, and you stood condemned in their eyes, with no hope of redeeming yourself? No one deserves that.

ATTEMPTS THAT DON'T WORK

Having said that, if you have gone through the diligent search and concluded, along with safe and sane people, that you really do have a button-pusher on your hands, then you are now ready to look at the following ways people deal with them ineffectively and see if you can identify yourself in any of them.

Reasoning with the Unreasonable

Probably the most common error is to believe that it's all about reason and logic, a meeting of the minds. You think that if the difficult person truly understands that what you are asking for is a good thing, he will comply and change. It is a matter of explaining the situation so that he can see what you are saying clearly. So you patiently attempt to explain how you feel, what you observe, and what you would like to happen. You may give examples of this so that the button-pusher can see it clearly.

So you might say, "Mike, your constant anger and putdowns of me are really hard on me. They make me feel bad about myself, and I don't like what they are doing to us. I think if you'd be more positive and affirming, I would appreciate it, and we'd have a better relationship."

Mike then says, "There you go again, I never get it right, do I? You're the one who puts me down."

You respond with, "No, that's not true. I just want you to be less critical, and I think that would help us."

Mike: "You're always pointing a finger at me."

You: "No, I'm not; I'm just trying to point out a problem."

Mike: "Yeah, but you're the problem. I wouldn't do these things if you weren't coming down on me all the time."

You: "No, no, it's not all me, Mike . . .," and the dance continues.

If this sounds familiar, there is good and bad news. The good news is that we should all begin with love, reason, and patience. Reasonable people respond to reason. That probably works for you, and perhaps most of your friends. So reason isn't the bad guy here.

The bad news is that an unreasonable person often will not listen to reason. Button-pushers have often constructed a world in their minds in which they have concluded they are right about their behavior, and what you say has little bearing. It is not as if he is thinking, *I could be going about this the wrong way . . . hmmm, she's got a good point about my criticism. I never thought about that.* Instead, he is hearing you like the old cartoon about what a dog hears when you scold him for messing up the carpet: *Blah blah blah Spot blah blah blah blah Spot blah blah blah.*

It is not about having more information, facts, or clarity. It is that you disagree, which in the button-pusher's mind is a signal to tune you out.

I have seen parents try to correct their child—I am not joking here—*while he or she was wearing a Walkman.* The child sits there, watches his parent's mouth moving, waits until it stops, and then keeps listening to the tunes. That's what is often happening, metaphorically speaking, while you are patiently coming up with just the right things to say!

So try reason; it's always a good start. But don't be like the Alcoholics Anonymous definition of insanity, which is trying the same thing over and over again, expecting a different result. If several attempts at reason break down, go on to the next things, which are in the next section of the book.

Splitting Grace and Truth

No one can change without having both grace and truth. Let's look at these two critical components of growth.

Grace is, as the classical theologians have defined it, *unmerited favor*. It is the most important ingredient of growth. It conveys God's favors and helps to us: "Let your conversation be always full of grace, seasoned with salt, so that you may know how to answer everyone" (Colossians 4:6).

Truth, on the other hand, is about *what is, what is real*. It comes from feedback, principles, Scripture, and consequences. It provides encouragement, answers, insight, and correction: "Buy the truth and do not sell it; get wisdom, discipline, and understanding" (Proverbs 23:23).

Grace and truth need each other. Truth operates to protect grace and love in the same way that your skeletal frame protects your heart. These must be in tandem: Grace gives us the fuel to live, grow, and change; truth protects and structures the process.

When we split grace and truth so that they are not integrated together in our relationships, things break down. Here is an example of how this works in parenting a teen. (Believe it or not, an adolescent can truly be a button-pusher!)

I was having dinner with Bob and Katie, a couple who are friends of ours. They were talking about their problems with Sarah, their adolescent daughter.

Sarah was a very bright, attractive, and fun young lady, but her antics were driving Bob and Katie to distraction. She had always been a handful, but when adolescence hit, things grew exponentially. Her grades were dropping dramatically. She was hanging with the wrong crowd. She was lying to her parents and sneaking out at night. Her attitude toward them and her siblings was atrocious. They were pulling their hair out.

I said, "Well, before we get to some solutions, let's talk about what you have been doing so far. That should give us some background."

Katie began: "I've really been trying to encourage Sarah. I think she feels bad about herself, and she needs to build some positive self-esteem. So when she makes a mistake, I hear her out and try to listen to what her experience is like. I want her to know that she is loved and safe. And a lot of the times she has shown me that there are some very good reasons for the problems that aren't her fault. Like her teacher this year is pretty cold and doesn't understand her. And she lost her watch, so she doesn't know what time it is when she's late. And she's trying to help the boy she's going out with, because he comes from a bad home and that's why he's on drugs."

I asked, "So how is that going?"

Katie said, "I think we're really making some progress. She trusts me and she opens up to me. Communication is the key, and I hope this will help her get motivated."

Bob weighed in with his analysis: "Sure, she talks to you. She knows you won't give her consequences, and you'll be sympathetic. No disrespect intended, but you've been doing this for a year now, and nothing has really changed, except that she likes you."

I said, "I suppose that counts for something, though. OK, what about you, Bob?"

"I am on Sarah's side too, just like Katie is, but Sarah is totally working the system here and at school. She manipulates everybody, has excuses for everything, and gets away with it all. I think she needs some discipline and consequences. So I don't even listen to the excuses anymore. I tell her the expectations and what will happen if she doesn't follow up. We need for her to see that she has to get her act together. "

"So how is your approach going?"

Now it was Katie's turn to evaluate Bob's approach: "Let's see . . . she avoids you, she won't open up to you, and she's afraid of you. She spent an hour with me last night crying because she thinks you hate her."

I totally understood and empathized with both of them. It was a pretty typical parenting scenario. Katie, whose family had been cold and overstrict, was giving Sarah what she herself had needed. She wasn't aware of how differently they had raised Sarah, and how Sarah already felt safe and loved. Sarah had had a childhood much better than Katie had had. She wasn't as fragile and bruised as Katie had been as a child. Bob, on the other hand, had had uninvolved parents and had gone too wild as an adolescent. He saw his own past coming up to haunt him in Sarah. He had needed structure and limits, and had suffered because of their nonexistence. So he was overboard on control and limits.

Bob and Katie both had a point in their approaches. But not only was each approach not working, they were polarized against each other. The result was that even the good they were doing was cancelled out by the other person. It was a classic case of one half plus one half equals zero. Katie was rescuing Sarah, and Bob was negated because he wasn't listening.

I said, "Guys, you're great people, and I love you and Sarah. But if we're going to make progress here, you both need to clear the deck of your approaches and be very open that you are both wrong. You've both been working very hard for a long time and doing a lot of good things. But I think we need to start all over again and come up with something that works.

Fortunately, Bob and Katie were good folks and humble enough to love Sarah more than being married to their biases. We worked on some of the principles in this book, and things did improve over time. They didn't want Sarah to be an adult button-pusher, and they are committed to helping her grow up to be a grown-up.

The problem comes in when you split, rather than integrate, grace and truth.[2] Like Bob and Katie, you become ineffective when you don't have enough of each. When your button-pusher receives all grace and no truth, he may feel loved, but also he may feel no reason to change. When he experiences all truth and no grace, he will feel condemnation and judgment, and likely react against it. Learn to have both grace and truth, love and reality, in every approach, every conversation, and every thought you have with your button-pusher.

Enabling

This is an often-used approach, because it is akin to, and even driven by, love for the button-pusher. *To enable, or rescue, someone is to remove the pain of that person's dysfunction from his experience.* It happens in any number of ways. You can avoid confronting him. You can provide comfort, warmth, and support for him even when he is being destructive. You can cover for him with his friends and family. You can pay his rent when he refuses to work. When he is unkind, you can blame yourself for provoking him.

Yet the enabler often believes in her heart that she is doing the right thing. She doesn't want him to feel pain because she doesn't want to see him hurt. She thinks that perhaps if he sees what she is doing for him, he will turn and change his ways. She hopes to turn him around with her love and care.

Again, love and care are wonderful things, and your button-pusher needs them if he is going to mend his behavior. However, and this is very important, *love and enabling are not the same thing*. Love does not promote irresponsibility. Love can be loving, and still have a zero tolerance toward button-pushing, control, selfishness, and manipulation. Enabling, on the other hand, takes on the responsibility of the button-pusher's problem, thus giving the enabler a double problem, and the difficult person, none.

I have a friend who had enabled her boss's irresponsibility for years. She took extra work when he forgot to get to it, covered for his mistakes, and generally rescued him into success. She genuinely liked him; he was a likeable guy, but a flaky one. Then, when he was promoted, they no longer worked together. His next assistant wasn't so accommodating. It was not long before his incompetence was uncovered and he lost his job. After that, my friend often wished that she had done something else before then, and maybe he would have changed. We'll never know, but we do know that enabling only protects a button-pusher from growing up and becoming a person of character.

If you suspect that you are enabling your button-pusher, it may help to know that *while you think you are caring, you are helping to ruin his life*. In effect, you are hating him. There is some pain that he may need to experience in order for the lights to go on. The right kinds of pain may do a lot to help.

Nagging, Err . . . Reminding

A close cousin to the reasoning approach, nagging (we call it reminding, or in even more polite circles, sharing) assumes that the person just needs to be reminded to do the right thing, that's all. When you think about it, it makes no sense, but we still do it. Does your button-pusher need to be reminded to eat breakfast, go to the mall, or look at TV? If he does, he may not be a button-pusher, he may have a neurological disorder! But we don't really think about it. Nagging is just a habit that we do.

Nagging isn't something most people employ with a rageaholic or defensive person. It is reserved more for the irresponsible or avoidant person who doesn't get to what they should be doing. For example, I have a friend whose husband nagged her to pay the bills on time. He calendared when the bills were due, twice a month, and would remind her a few days beforehand to do them. This is a grown professional woman we are talking about. He did this for years, and it wasn't until he quit and she started having to pay late fees that things began to change.

The problem is, nagging isn't just ineffective, it ultimately makes things worse. This is because you often symbolically become the parent that the button-pusher is attempting to separate from. Thus, you are perceived as controlling and authoritarian. So the button-pusher reverts to a childish state and rebels against the parent by increasing the bad behavior. You see this in a lot of marriages and dating relationships. The love, trust, and passion deteriorate quickly when two adults become a kid and a parent.

Threatening with No Follow-up

Just don't ever do this. Don't.

Threatening is often a move of desperation by the person who sees no change in the button-pusher. It's the last straw, and an attempt to get her attention. You may threaten anything from emotionally distancing to removing privileges to leaving. The thinking is that the shock value will get through to her, and she will get her act together and become more responsive, more loving, less blaming, or whatever.

Certainly warnings can be a good thing. That is what yellow stoplights and blood pressure readings are for. They say, *Listen to this or something bad is going to happen.* They can save our lives. But warning and threatening without following up on what we say is ruinous.

Threatening is more than ineffective. It actually makes things worse. When you deliver empty or even inconsistent threats, *you are training your button-pusher to ignore you.* You are saying, in effect, "I'm going to blow off steam now. If you will sit tight and wait it out, you can go back to doing whatever you were doing, and nothing will happen to you." It's a button-pusher's dream: a small price to pay for the total freedom to say or do whatever she wants. We will deal more with follow-up when we discuss taking action in chapter 10.

I had a man tell me once about his girlfriend who had blown up at him for his inappropriate flirting, "It's OK, she's all bark and no bite." He was even a little proud that he had figured her out so well. He was dead on. And obviously, he did not feel any need to change his hurtfulness.

So if you bark, be prepared to bite. If you aren't, get yourself a muzzle!

Our Own Denial

The button-pusher is not the only person who is avoiding looking at his life. Often, the other individual in the equation is as well. You may be in some denial about the nature or gravity of the problem. When we deny, we actually distort reality. It is a mechanism that shifts our perception of a painful thing to see it as not there at all, or not as bad as it truly is.

Denial isn't all bad. Trauma and catastrophe victims sometimes need it to be able to slow down assimilating the horror of what has happened to them, so that they will not be overwhelmed with the emotions and memories. But normally, denial simply keeps our head in the sand, wishing and hoping that things aren't as bad as they are.

So you may find that you minimize your button-pusher's hurtful, annoying, or selfish actions. You may say to yourself or others, *He has so many good qualities;* or *He's just having a bad day;* or *If I hadn't burned the toast, he wouldn't have said that.* There is certainly nothing wrong with looking at positive things, but there is a lot wrong with avoiding negative realities. They do not vanish when we avoid them, and they often get worse.

We deny for the same reasons button-pushers do: fear of loss of love; not wanting to appear or be bad; avoidance of conflict, guilt, or pride, for example. These are real issues, and can be dealt with in the proper growth or help contexts, such as a structured support group or counseling. But denial can rob you of life and years, so it is worth it to work through it and see reality as it is. Reality is always your friend.

A good antidote to denial, if you find yourself doing this, is to go to a safe, trusted, and truthful friend who knows your situation. Safe people want the best for you, even if it means experiencing some present unpleasantness for a future success. Ask them if you are avoiding the seriousness of your button-pusher's situation. They may tell you that it is truly a bad problem, and that may free you to take the needed actions.[3]

Remember Cindy, who denied how severe Dylan's condition was? She was protecting herself against the sadness that the son she loved was not a good person, at least at that point in his life. You can understand how she would not want to look at that. But when she had accepted it, she was then able to truly help Dylan in the ways that meant something.

One Time Should Do It

One of the things I hear over and over again on the national radio show I co-host goes like this:

> "I have a problem person in my life."
> "OK, tell me about the situation."
> "My husband drinks too much and lies to me."
> "That's a bad problem. What have you done so far about it?"
> "I told him I wanted him to stop."
> "Did he?"
> "No."
> "So what then?"
> "Well, I gave up then. He didn't stop. Should I leave him?"

This sort of person with a button-pusher has the "one time should do it" approach. This means that she hopes and expects that one appeal, or confrontation, or invitation, or threat, or consequence, should be enough. If it doesn't work, then she gets discouraged and resigns herself to a bad situation.

This type of thinking is driven by several things: a fear of wading into conflict or not having the ability to be in conflict; a lack of resources and help to pull it off; or wishful thinking. But it isn't realistic or effective.

Forget the button-pushers for a minute—most of the healthy people I know need more than one reminder! I know that I do. I wish it weren't true, but it is. So, *it is better to look at change and growth as things that happen over a process of time, and not as an event.* It isn't the one event that can change your button-pusher; it is a series of events, thought out and executed with wisdom, love, and support.

Spiritualizing

It is a good thing, perhaps the best thing, for you and your button-pusher to be spiritual people. But it can be the worst thing for you to be a spiritualizing person.

To be spiritual is to live in relationship to God and his ways: "God is spirit, and his worshipers must worship in spirit and in truth" (John 4:24). To do so means a life of obedience, faith, love, and mystery. Spiritual people know that humbly following God is the best way to live. However, to *spiritualize* is to distort true spirituality. The term refers to the practice of using spiritual concepts to defend against some negative reality. The end result is that God often gets blamed for a person's character issues.

There are three major spiritualizations people do with their button-pusher. The first is *preaching*. Here they repeatedly and ineffectively try to motivate the difficult person by telling him Bible verses or principles that have helped them. There is great gain to be had by heeding Scripture. However, if a person is not open to it or responding, it is sometimes wiser to, instead of preaching the Word, *actually live the Word* with your person: becoming the most loving, fun, responsible, honest person possible. This can sometimes help a person see the value of the Scriptures toward a good life.

Secondly, some people become *passive*. That is, they withdraw from doing anything to solve the problem, and simply pray and hope. This, to them, is sometimes their own last resort when all else has failed. It is a good thing to stop playing God and to ask him to do the job he does. But that never removes our responsibility to do the jobs he asks us to do. We are co-laborers with him, and he often shows people things to do with their button-pushers that are in addition to prayer.

The most destructive spiritualization, however, is *superiority*. In this attitude, the person feels so close to God that she can no longer relate to the earthly ways of her button-pusher. She cares, but from a distance, because he does not understand the spiritual truths that she lives in her experience.

This is a dangerous perch to rest on. It is rooted in pride and is not truly spiritual at all. Spiritual people understand the daily grace they need to deal with the issues and darkness within their own souls. They are on their face before God, asking his help to work through these things, and they are contrite and grateful to him. They do not see themselves as above or below anyone; rather, they are more concerned with connecting to God and people in good, healthy, and growing ways.

So get rid of spiritualizing, and ask God to make you spiritual. You stand a much better chance of being a change agent for your button-pusher.

Taking Too Much Responsibility

It is easy to quickly assume that the difficult person's negative effects are not because of her character and choices, but because you are doing something wrong. Perhaps she is unreliable and undependable. You stopped asking her to get something from the grocery store a long time ago because you know you'll get home and it won't be there.

But when you say something about it, she says that it's because your demands are too much with all the other responsibilities she bears. You are the straw that broke her back. And if you tend toward being overly responsible in the first place, this sort of scenario can cause you to see yourself as the provocateur and the problem.

There is no question that we should all scrutinize our lives and actions to see if we are doing what we are confronted with. But having done that, we need to investigate to see if there is a pattern for taking on too much of a burden of the problem brought about by the button-pusher.

This problem also manifests itself when we take ownership for fixing the button-pusher. That is, we put ourselves in charge of the difficult person's choices and the outcome. This is often due to some lack of personal definition and separateness. The best balance is to work hard on your end of things and to leave the outcome to your person and to God.

Waiting for Permission

There is a polite, hopeful part in all of us that is somewhat conflict-avoidant. And it operates a little like movies of the old days in England, where manners and etiquette were everything: you wait politely until the button-pusher is ready and open to being helped, and then, and only then, do you speak up. Hopefully, he will see the errors of his ways and come to you to help him change.

It can be a long wait. Often, the last thing the difficult person wants to do is to ask someone to help him change. The more silence there is, the more assent he perceives and assumes. While the individual may not want to appear controlling or intrusive, the result is that things escalate and get out of control.

I worked with a woman once who thought that her silence and withdrawal would be enough so that her impulsive spendaholic husband would notice and ask what was wrong. They were almost bankrupt before I convinced her that her plan was not working.

Politeness and not being controlling are good things. But there is also a place for warning, interrupting a problem, and confronting, both in season and out of season (2 Timothy 4:2), that is, when the person is open, and sometimes when he is not.

Reacting and Blasting

Let's all confess together now: *I let my button-pusher push me to say stuff I wish I'd never said.* As we saw in the introduction, your person can influence you to be someone you don't want to be, and draw out your lower nature in a way that can be surprising. I have seen missionary ladies, when triggered by someone in their life, come out with vocabulary I don't think they even knew they knew. And button-pushers can evoke intense feelings of love, anger, helplessness, and anxiety.

This capacity to react and blast away is due to some dependency we have. That is, we are in a need state for something, perhaps warmth, affirmation, or love; and we look for it from the difficult person. Then, when it is not forthcoming, we don't respond maturely, but in desperation and high emotion. Sometimes it is done to try to change the person and get their attention, sort of a *look-what-you've-driven-me-to* thinking. But generally, it is very ineffective. The button-pusher more often than not thinks, *See? I'm not the problem; that crazy, raving person is.*

If your button-pusher does not provide you with something you need, find a safe and sane place to get it, at least for now. There are people around who have capacities for respect, help, and empathy, and you need to find ways to avail yourself of them.

I've Tried Everything . . .

This approach is not actually an approach. It is more of a resistance. However, it is a common attitude that deserves to be discussed. The individual has attempted many things and has found that nothing changes the button-pusher. She feels hopeless and helpless and sees no good end to the matter, only that things will remain the same.

In theory, it is possible that a person *has* tried everything with her button-pusher, but it is only theory. Most of the time I have found that it means something else. It often means that the person has tried some of the ineffective things in this chapter, which are doomed to fail. Or it means that she has tried a few good things, but not enough of them. Or she has made attempts, but without enough support or persistence.

In section 3, we will present several key resources to help you create a change environment for your button-pusher. You may find that you are doing some, but there are some that you weren't aware of. And sometimes it means that the person has done a little bit of some good things, like the "one time should do it" person. They stuck their toe in the water and drew it back too soon.

So, clear the deck of these ineffective approaches and, in the next chapter, begin to think of these principles in relation to your vision of helping your button-pusher to change.

Developing a Vision for Change:
Your Personal Starting Point

WHEN I COUNSEL PEOPLE about their button-pusher, I
will often ask them what their vision is for the future of
the relationship. Many times, the answer is a quizzical
look as if I'm speaking Martian. The look is then followed by something like, "What are you talking about? I just want to survive this
person and not go crazy. There's your vision."

It is understandable that those in a difficult relationship have
trouble with the concept of vision. The word has to do with positive
things in life like high goals, dreams, and shared aspirations. Large
companies often begin with a dream. Churches and ministries have
the same origins. Humble beginnings but lofty goals—that's the
nature of vision. Those with a button-pusher don't feel the same
creative, energetic brainstorming freedom. They are too busy playing defense, warding off the effects of the relationship, worrying,
and, as in the earlier conversation, sometimes just trying to survive.

To put it in a metaphor, it's hard to have a vision in the middle of a nightmare.

Why You Need a Vision

At the same time, however, you do need a vision, especially if you are in a button-pushing relationship. This goes far beyond survival. For you to embrace and use the seven resources available to you, you will need to do things you haven't done before, or are afraid of, or that are unpleasant for you, yet are the necessary things. And vision helps you sustain the effort and courage required.

This is especially important in difficult relationships, as there is generally some resistance, or even escalation, in the other person when you begin to make the important changes that must occur. You need a place inside yourself to keep you on track.

Let's briefly describe vision as *a mental picture of a desired outcome which gives you heart and focus*. It is an image you have crafted and constructed in your mind that encapsulates the goal you have. Its purpose is to carry you through the dark times so that you can see them through to completion. People who want to lose weight might put a photo of a bathing suit that they want to get into on the refrigerator. Those saving for a home might have a diagram of the dream house on the wall. An individual working for a job promotion may have a desk plate with his name and the position engraved on it.

Vision is given by God and is modeled by him. One of Jesus' final statements on the cross was "It is finished" (John 19:30). The "it" was his vision to redeem the world to himself by enduring death for us, and he completed his mission. That is the nature of vision. When circumstances are the stormiest, clarity of vision has kept many a sojourner steadily on the path.

In the introduction to the book, we painted a vision for the goals of the book. This chapter describes a different sort of vision. This is a particular, specific, and individual vision, tailored to your situation with your button-pusher.

ASPECTS OF VISION

How do you go about creating a vision for what you want to see? Here are some ideas to try out.

Presence of the Good versus Absence of the Bad

This is a hard one. It's difficult to see beyond a desire for a husband to stop yelling and throwing things, or for a wife to lay off the constant nagging. These involve the cessation of bad things, which is certainly important, but that's not enough. If all that happens is that a bad behavior ends, you are probably selling yourself short. Far better to want him to be approachable and able to deal with conflict lovingly, and for her to be patient and vulnerable when there is a problem.

Put a Relational Component into Your Vision

You are most likely in a personal relationship with your button-pusher. That is, you would like what any of us would like from her: relational components such as closeness, safety, intimacy, respect, freedom, trust, and mutuality. These are important, as relationship is the greatest part of life. Paint these into your vision.

AIM HIGH

You may be discouraged, but still aim high in your vision. As the old saying goes, Aim at a star and you may hit a stump; aim at a stump and you may hit nothing at all. People with low expectations are rarely disappointed, and that is not a good thing.

There is a range of vision that applies to the button-pushing relationship. The highest road is that your difficult person will be transformed from the inside out. That vision involves much more than changed behavior; it involves a changed heart. And it integrates the external behaviors, troublesome though they be, with the internal world, which is a more thorough and complete process. Here are some examples of high aims for your difficult individual.

- The irresponsible wife who is financially ruining the family matures and becomes dependable and reliable.

- The self-centered friend who will not pay attention to your feelings and concerns develops the ability to put others before himself and have genuine and deep empathy.

- The heavy-drinking husband will not only stop drinking, but will resolve the emotional pain inside that makes it difficult to be around him.

- The moody adult child whose outbursts cause chaos becomes stable, kind, and fun to be around.

- The controlling boss demonstrates grace and freedom to his subordinates.

All Things Are Possible

Try not to be too skeptical at this point! You may very well be thinking, *This is not reality and is not possible*. I agree that when it comes to human freedom, there are few guarantees. But there are two guarantees that are important to know. One is that all things are possible with God (Matthew 19:26); and the second is that God is on your side, and he has designed your button-pusher to be better off and happier when he is doing life God's way.

So put skepticism on the back burner for now, and work on crafting your own vision.

The Bottom Line

Never forget what we discussed in chapter 1 as you are developing your mental image: most of the time, the problem of all problems in a button-pusher is that he does not own, or take responsibility for, the issues that affect his life and those around him.

This must be in place here: your vision must include the picture of this person being able to be open to being wrong, to being sorry, to hearing how he affects you, to seeing himself as the contributor to the problem, and to entering a process of change to help him if needed. When this line is crossed, and it may not be instantaneous, everything speeds up and goes better.

WHAT WILL YOU SETTLE FOR?

You will also need some sort of minimum requirement. That is, you will need to clearly articulate the smallest sort of change you will accept as being a good thing. A husband who doesn't withdraw and sulk for weeks, but who still won't get into a growth group to look at his issues, is still better for you than one who hasn't changed at all. A wife who overspends a lot less than she did, but still overspends, is an improvement. An alcoholic who stops drinking from willpower alone is no longer a danger to himself or others for now, though he runs a relapse risk and often manifests irritability or depressions that the drinking has been masking.

By no means am I saying that you are to be satisfied and content with external restraint that involves no internal shifts of attitude, feeling, perspective, and value. That can, and should, be a lifelong desire and goal. At the same time, however, stay away from chronic criticism of the other person. You don't want your button-pusher living under your *not enough* mantra. He will ultimately rebel against it, and you both lose. A better stance than that is, *This is good, and I want even better for us*.

This is also important because if you just get changed behavior without a changed life, that is certainly progress, but the changes are vulnerable to being very temporary if everything stops there. Almost any school kid can keep from shooting spit wads when the teacher is in the room. But the impulsive ones can't stop when she is away. You want your difficult person's insides to change so that he doesn't want to do the bad things he has been doing.

Always keep your vision focused on heart change. It is the deepest, most permanent, and most effective. And it takes the longest amount of time to change, but that's the nature of change and growth.

ADD THE DETAILS

When a button-pusher changes, life changes. The relationship becomes a place in which things you thought would never happen can now happen. Think about people you know who have a good relationship, and the good things they are able to do. Put these in too. That may mean anything from more time together, to travel or starting some sort of help or ministry to struggling people, to hobbies, arts, or sports. These add-ons help your courage, perseverance, and focus.

PART THREE

Implementing
Your Resources

5

RESOURCE #1: GOD

I F THERE IS ANYTHING IN THE WORLD that will get a person thinking about God, it is a difficult relationship. It can put you straight down on your knees.

We need good relationships to survive, and we are designed by God for a relational purpose. People matter to us, and when the love or companionship we want encounters problems and disconnections, it is difficult to ignore the pain and discomfort of it. Furthermore, since we are pretty much helpless to control another person's actions or words, we are forced to confront our own powerlessness. And the experience of powerlessness is often a direct route to looking toward God.

When I speak to people in conferences around the world, I hear, over and over again, that many of them began to turn to God as a result of a problem relationship. I was speaking recently at a gathering on spiritual and emotional growth, and I asked the attendees to raise their hands as to which reason they had come to the conference. Was it emotional issues or behavioral issues, work-related, a general spiritual quest for growth, or a relationship problem? The great majority chose relationship problems. Marriages, dating, family, the work environment, and friendships can all elicit the experience that *we have come to the end of ourselves.*

It makes sense: you care about a button-pusher and want things to go well between the two of you. Yet that person is free to choose his behavior toward you, his attitudes, and whether he even wants to be in the relationship with you. Loving someone is truly a dilemma. Loving a difficult person can be very, very tough.

God Gets It

God understands this situation. He knows it conceptually, and he knows it in experience. God lives in it every day, caring about us and just wanting a relationship with us that is for our best; yet he gives us the freedom to say no to him, which we often do.

Jesus' words to the people illustrate the depth of his emotion and empathy toward us:

> O Jerusalem, Jerusalem, you who kill the prophets and stone those sent to you, how often I have longed to gather your children together, as a hen gathers her chicks under her wings, but you were not willing." (Matthew 23:37–38)

God desires the connection profoundly, yet he does not violate the free will that he also created within us. He allows himself to experience that sort of tension, not because it is good or pleasant for him, but because *freedom is the only way that we will ever have a relationship that comes from within—from the heart—and is not forced or controlled.* That is the only sort of relationship he is interested in, and ultimately it is the best way we are to relate to him and each other.

HIS INVESTMENT IN YOUR BUTTON-PUSHER

As we have seen earlier, button-pushers can be complicated people who create complicated relationships. Yet God shines the light of truth and understanding on these matters. He is the one who "knows the secrets of the heart" (Psalm 44:21). He is aware of the inconsistencies, the sudden mood shifts, the counterattacks and blaming, and all the things in your difficult person that mystify you. These are not mysteries to him; rather, he can point the way through the mazes.

That is why putting God as your first resource in dealing with your button-pusher is not about being "religious." It has nothing to do with that. It is about submitting to and following reality, wisdom, support, and guidance. When you encounter a problem in normal life—something you have little experience with—most people call an expert and consult someone with experience. Physicians are for medical things, accountants for tax matters, and teachers are for educational issues. Literally, *God has more experience dealing with button-pushers than anyone*. And he knows the answers to any question or situation about dealing with difficult people. Going to the Architect of Relationships is not just a spiritual thing; it is based on reality.

The Plan of Reconciliation

God has an intent and plan for your button-pusher, just as he does for you. That intent is *reconciliation*. Reconciliation is the process whereby estranged parties resolve their differences and become allied again. He wants your difficult person to be reconciled to God himself, to others, and to his own heart. It is one of the things that God is most interested in for humanity: ". . . God was reconciling the world to himself in Christ, not counting men's sins against them. And he has committed to us the message of reconciliation" (2 Corinthians 5:19).

If your button-pusher is doing the things you see him doing, it generally indicates that at least one of those three areas of reconciliation may not be operating. The person may not be fully connected to God and his life. He is certainly not reconciled with you and probably others. And he likely has parts of himself that are not reconciled with other parts, which puts his life in conflict, especially in relationships. One of the best things you can do is to ask God to reconcile your person in those three areas of life and relationship.

On the Button-Pusher's Team

It is also important to realize that God is "for" your difficult person, just as he is "for" you. He deeply wants the best possible life for the button-pusher, which is good to know, especially when you have run out of love and good wishes and feel little but negative emotions toward him. God is an inexhaustible reservoir of grace and love, not only in order to help you to hang in there with your person, but also to come directly from himself to the person. I have often prayed in my life, "God, I am out of love for this person; sorry about that. Please give me some of yours, because there's no more in here." And he has done that.

This certainly doesn't mean that God agrees with the stances and behaviors of your button-pusher. He may be more on your side than his with regard to what the person is doing. God takes clearly defined positions on many issues, such as deception (Psalm 101:7), lack of love (Matthew 24:12), selfishness (James 3:16), and irresponsibility (Proverbs 20:4). But as Creator, Father, and Redeemer, he loves and wants good things for him.

THE ARCHITECT OF LIFE AND RELATIONSHIPS

But there is more to looking to God than simply knowing that he cares and understands the situation. There are practical and functional reasons also. He is the Architect of Relationships. He designed the nature of human connections, in all its complexity, and how the connections work. He is relationship itself.

In his role as Architect, God mapped out life and relationships according to certain rules and laws that operate in certain ways. As he does not fail, neither do his laws. When we live in submission to them, life tends to work better. When we are antagonistic to them, things should, and do, break down. Just like physical laws of magnetism, gravity, and electricity, you can't really fight them for very long. Try to say that you don't believe in or agree with gravity, and jump up. You may do some hang time, but even Michael Jordan had to come down sooner or later.

Take the law of sowing and reaping, derived from Galatians 6:7: "Do not be deceived: God cannot be mocked. A man reaps what he sows." The basic idea is that for every cause there is an effect; for every action there is a consequence. If we sow love, humility, and responsibility, we should reap those. If we fail to sow these, we should experience disconnection, reactions to our pride, and losses.[1]

A button-pusher who sows selfishness and arrogance should, in a real and practical way, have people giving him all sorts of grief. His family should be confronting him. His friends should be telling him that they are going to stay away until he shows he cares about something besides himself. His boss should be holding back his promotion because he bugs his co-workers. I have seen the law of sowing and reaping work in powerful ways when people allowed the button-pusher to experience it. Conversely, I have seen it interrupted by well-meaning rescuers and enablers, and its power gets temporarily nullified by those willing to help the person avoid the consequences. God chastises those whom he loves (Hebrews 12:6). Do not make the mistake of getting between your difficult person and God's rules.

In the same vein, your difficult person should notice an improvement in life when he becomes caring, self-controlled, and honest. You and others should warm to him; people should affirm him and want to be around him; work should go better. All this is to say that God and his ways are bigger, larger, and stronger than your button-pusher. He must feel the pressure of the way life runs and operates. Though he certainly has the freedom to shake his fist at God, the world, and you, he cannot forever avoid the effects of the way the universe has been designed.

Ask God to place you in the right position to be part of the growth, or sanctification, process for your button-pusher. He is operating behind the scenes, and though the fields are white for harvest, there is a labor shortage (Matthew 9:37–38). Sign up as a volunteer to help God help your button-pusher. He may tell you to confront something, or to stop nagging, or to deal with some blindness in yourself. Whatever he says, however, it is for you, the person, and the relationship.

THE MESSAGE BEHIND THE CRAZINESS

In a deeper way, be aware also that God may be doing something behind the scenes with you, in and through your button-pushing relationship. He may be working with you to get to know him (that is, God) better also. God is not very interested in solving your relationship problem simply in order that you become a happy person. He knows that is not ultimately best for you. Happiness should not be a goal in life; it is a byproduct of something else, and that is being connected to him and his life. God does not want to be your Prozac. He wants *you.* "If anyone hears my voice and opens the door, I will come in and eat with him, and he with me" (Revelation 3:20).

Often the button-pushing relationship will help us grow spiritually, as well as being more connected to God. We learn about faith as unseen realities are happening in the relationship. We learn about hope as we desire to see change that only God can bring about in the future. We learn about love as we see how much he wants to help us and our difficult person.

I have a friend who is married to a former button-pusher. (Yes, that happens, and quite often!) She was already deeply into her faith and relationship with God, but the struggles she went through in her marriage changed her in ways that have been profound and permanent. For example, her view of pain is now one of embracing it. She does not enjoy pain, but she does not turn from any pain that might cause her to grow spiritually and personally. She sees God behind it, and moves toward it.

You may be praying and asking God for guidance, and that is a good thing. It may be something like, "God, help me to know how to best handle my person." I would suggest you add to that prayer the following: "God, help me see what lesson you want me to learn from all this about my life with you. Help me see it's not just about changing him but about transforming me." God's realities work for us all. He is integrated with his truths, and they are universal. What is good for your button-pusher is good for you also.

There may be a faith journey ahead for you underneath the turmoil of your difficult relationship. Look for it.

Faith a la Abraham

How do you fit God, yourself, and your button-pusher all together in faith? There are several elements involved, best illustrated in the life of Abraham, who is called the Father of Faith. He left his familiar surroundings and followed God in faith, as you will have to do.

> By faith Abraham, when called to go to a place he would later receive as his inheritance, obeyed and went, even though he did not know where he was going. By faith he made his home in the promised land like a stranger in a foreign country; he lived in tents, as did Isaac and Jacob, who were heirs with him of the same promise. For he was looking forward to the city with foundations, whose architect and builder is God. (Hebrews 11:8–10)

Abraham was called. This is something God has done for many years with his people. He extends himself to us in many, many ways. Faith is about recognizing the call. The call may be in the form of a burning bush, a Bible verse that jumps off the page, a conversation on the phone, or an email from a friend. The important thing here is to be open and attend. Pay attention; listen for the call.

Attending is not easy in a world of pagers, cell phones, and instant messaging. You will probably need to find some structured minutes in your day in order to hear the still small voice within the din of modern life.

During this time, confess to God you are at the end of your resources with your button-pusher; you have done everything you know, and he is not responding. Ask him for help, and let him know that you are open to any way he responds and any direction he says. Make it truly *Thy will, not my will.* This only makes sense, as your solutions have not helped you. It is truly time to listen to another voice.

Calls vary by nature and by situation. Your call may be to do nothing right now about your button-pusher but to sit tight and get connected to God. Or it may be to change the way you are oper-ating with your person. Keep an open mind.

Abraham went to a place he didn't know. He chose to go in faith, without attempting to control the situation. He landed in unfamil-iar territory, in a foreign land. This was out of his comfort zone.

You might think, *I am not in a comfort zone either,* but that is not true. You may be unhappy or miserable in your relationship, but *there is comfort in the known bad.* You may know how to manage the person by walking on eggshells around him. You may have learned how to predict his moods. You may have figured out how to protect the finances from his irresponsibility. You may know when to avoid him when he's having a bad day. And that may work, in a survival mode sort of way. There is comfort in these structures, and you probably needed them to cope. But it may be time for some new ways and approaches. I can pretty much assure you that growing in faith with your button-pusher will take you out of your comfort zone.

You may have to say things you are afraid to say, or do things you aren't used to doing. You may have to deal with some things inside yourself that are painful. But when you look at it realistically, what are the alternatives? They are reduced to returning to your old approaches, which haven't worked to change things, or to giving up, which may mean things might even get worse. That is the mystery of God: he takes situations that are at their worst, when we are at the end of our rope, and he gets involved. He redeems, repairs, restores, and heals. That is his nature: "'I will ransom them from the power of the grave; I will redeem them from death'" (Hosea 13:14).

Faith is all about getting out of the land of comfort. God just does not provide his help and love along with comfort. That is not how he does things. Sooner or later, he says to get out of the boat and start walking. So say goodbye to the comfort zone, listen to the call, and walk.

Abraham had a future hope. He lived in tents, but he looked forward to a city with foundations. "Foundations" refers to stability and strength. It is the hope of a future with peace and security. You will be living in a tent for a while—the tent of new experiences, relationships, thoughts, feelings, and risks. But there is a city waiting for you that you can look forward to. It is the city of a better life: the life of God, a life of relationship and freedom, and, hopefully, a life that sees your button-pusher enter the process of growth and change himself. That is worth a camping trip in a tent.

Faith in God, Not Faith in Faith

It is important that you understand that this life of faith is not about desiring or wishing. That puts the power in the hands of the wisher. The power of true faith is rooted in the substance and reality of the object of that faith. That object is God—your primary source for dealing with button-pushers—and no one can deal with them better than he. I have seen God do miracles with button-pushers over the past many years. People I would have never dreamed would take ownership over their behaviors have turned around. God's presence and his process of growth can be trusted. Get away from it all and listen for the call.

6

RESOURCE #2: YOUR LIFE

I'LL NEVER FORGET THE DAY I accidentally discovered the mystery behind Kevin and Cheryl's disconnect. I was seeing them in marital counseling, and they were a confusing couple. I couldn't understand the patterns between them. It seemed like it should be Cheryl in individual counseling, without Kevin, but she wanted him there, and he meekly agreed to come.

Cheryl was always overreactive and angry about the slightest infractions of Kevin's. It could be anything from forgetting to bring home milk to not turning off lights. I was siding pretty much against Cheryl on things, as it seemed Kevin was receiving a lot of undeserved heat. She was the button-pusher, in my book.

But that one day he came in late, and it wasn't the first time. I'm fairly strict about both people in couples work being on time, so I was going to say something about it. But Cheryl blew up, saying how inconsiderate Kevin was and how it was like their whole marriage. So I was thinking about how to address Cheryl when out of the corner of my eye, I noticed that Kevin was smiling. It wasn't a grin; it was smaller and more secretive, but it was definitely a smile.

"Kevin, you're smiling. What's up?" I asked.

At first he tried to deny it, but Cheryl had seen it too. Finally he admitted it. And what eventually came out was that it was sort of a *victory grin* for Kevin. This was a man who was invested in looking like the normal guy with the crazy wife. It was very important for him to appear OK, and her not OK. And, later, when he became very, very honest, he figured out that he was intentionally coming in just a few minutes late to our session, knowing that Cheryl would look like a rageaholic, and he would look like the victim. So really, he was the angry one, making her look angry.

I had bought that scenario until the smile happened. So I told Cheryl, "I understand your anger now. Kevin does set you up sometimes. I get it. But I must tell you that you will never have the marriage you want until you stop being so easily provoked by his covert actions. From now on, when you sense these little barbs from him, I want you to say to him, 'I feel disconnected and hurt. Was that on purpose or did I do something to make you mad? Would you tell me what it was, so we can reconnect?'"

Cheryl was awesome. She was able to move past her anger and into her hurt and vulnerability with Kevin. Eventually, her making the first move of health began to get to Kevin. He wasn't able to enjoy seeing her freak out, because she wasn't freaking out. She was just sad and hurt. He stopped trying to look like the good guy, and showed he had problems too. He couldn't hide his anger at her, so it was apparent that he was provoking on purpose. He became the angry one for a while, and we had to deal with that. He began to feel more empowerment as he became more direct, instead of feeling like a little boy making faces at the teacher behind her back. He started feeling like a man with her. And he began to discover empathy and care for his wife, and, ultimately, remorse for the pain he was causing her. The covert button-pusher changed in some substantial and deep ways. I don't think it would have happened had Cheryl not been able to move from frustration and reactivity to sadness and hurt. Her softness melted him.

I am summarizing a lot of work in a few words, but Kevin and Cheryl's case shows a point: *You and your life are an agent for change with your button-pusher.* The way you live, move, and operate in the world and the relationship has power that you may not be aware of. Certainly there are husbands who would not have been moved by Cheryl's change. But I have seen something similar to this case happen many times.

We don't often think of our life as being a resource to help change things with a button-pusher. We think more about conversations and actions, which we will deal with later. But you can influence and accomplish much by the way you live.

This can be explained as a matter of light and darkness. The more your life is in the light—that is, exposed fully to love, truth, and the growth process—the more you become light. The darkness and the hiding that the button-pusher is experiencing reacts to that light. He cannot stay neutral for long, as light and dark are not compatible. He is forced to change positions, one way or another. Either he finds himself uncomfortable with love, honesty, and growth, yet is drawn to it and begins to change, becoming a person of light himself. Or he senses that many things might have to change, so he becomes antagonistic toward the light and moves against it, or away from it. "The light shines in the darkness, but the darkness has not understood it" (John 1:5). Either way, there is movement, and that is good.

Moving toward your life of light helps your button-pusher grow, as with Kevin and Cheryl. And moving away from the light is a commitment that helps the person define her true character and motives. Better to know the bad news and help the person experience the consequences, than to have her pretend to be something she is not, which is a hopeless case.

Your life is like an oven of growth for the difficult person. You add gradual heat by being a good and growing person, and the individual experiences the heat. So look at these elements of a good life and begin to see how who you are, as you change and grow, can change the life of your button-pusher.

Reclaim Your Happiness from the Button-Pusher

One of the most powerful principles that helps people begin to see changes in their relationship involves retrieving, recapturing, and reclaiming control over their own happiness, which they have shifted to their button-pusher. It is very easy to feel that unless your person changes, you will be bereft of love, or frustrated, powerless, or unhappy. That is, the person holds the golden key to a major part of your life, and as long as he does not cooperate, your life suffers significantly.

This should not be limited to just button-pushing relationships, either. Even if all your relationships are good and sound, your happiness, growth, and well-being should be up to you, God, and your spiritual community, and not dependent on one single person. The Bible says that your life is your life, and you will be called to account for how you lived it. That is an individual accounting, not between you and another person: "So then, each of us will give an account of himself to God" (Romans 14:12). One of the hallmarks of an adult is that they have moved past childhood dependency on parents into adult dependency on support systems. Parents guard us, tell us what to do, and somewhat control us. Support systems give us love, truth, and modeling, but they don't make our decisions for us. Stay in charge of your own quest for a good and meaningful life.

For example, I talked to Amanda, a woman who had had a conflict with her best friend, Pam, and Pam had abruptly ended the relationship. Amanda had thought they had a strong relationship, so she was very surprised when Pam stopped calling and basically shut down the connection. This had happened several months before we talked, and yet Amanda's pain and emotions were still quite strong. Day in and day out Amanda couldn't get her friend out of her mind. Since Pam wouldn't give an explanation for the rift, Amanda was left with no closure, which made her feel guilty and confused. She even got somewhat obsessive about the problem, leaving messages and e-mails for Pam and talking to mutual friends about what happened. Basically, the absent friend was in control of her happiness and well being.

I told her, "You have a legitimate complaint, in that you need an answer from her to be able to make sense of things and let it go. But you need to let it go even with the loose ends, and move on. Make the lack of closure another aspect of your grief: you miss Pam, and you miss having answers and info. But move on."

Amanda was able to do that and let go of her obsessive behaviors. To my knowledge, Pam has never responded, but at least Amanda has retrieved her life through her grief and letting go.

If you have a button-pusher, you need to literally "get a life." In other words, it is important for you to develop the capacity to multitask in the relational world. You need to do two things at once: first, to be able to deal effectively and redemptively with your difficult person; and second, to be able to navigate a good and fulfilling life, no matter how the person is responding or not responding. That is the freedom you need, and you must do this.

Why We Give Away Ownership of Our Lives

It is the most natural thing in the world to allow your button-pusher to control your life and happiness in this manner, but it is not the best thing in the world. How do people get to this place? There are several reasons, and solutions.

Lack of awareness. Sometimes, gradually and over a period of time, a person will find that the center of life has become taken over by the button-pusher, or by some problem the difficult person is causing. Before this relationship, the person had meaning, interests, and good relationships. Then, as the button-pushing relationship developed, the center and focus of her life began to shift from inside herself to fixing and addressing the problem.

Since this happens gradually, you tend not to notice the change. When you are not aware of the situation, it is easy to see the relationship issue as simply one of life's several problems to solve. A lot of life involves handling difficulties, from the relational world to the financial, spiritual, and medical worlds. Most of the time you invest some time and energy, and many difficulties can be resolved in a successful way. If you have a work problem, you have a meeting with some people and fix it. If you have a relationship problem with a regular friend, you chat, discuss it, and work it out. But when you come up against the button-pusher's lack of ownership, things are different. "Normal" discussions, reasoning, entreaties, and nagging have little effect.

At that point, a strange transformation may have happened inside you. Instead of backing off and realizing you were up against a new and different problem, you began to work harder and harder, giving up more and more territory in your life, bringing more and more friends into the equation, and so forth. You read an article in a magazine and think, *Maybe that will help*. You read a Bible verse and bring it to your button-pusher's attention, hoping his eyes will be opened. You start asking lots of people for advice.

There is nothing wrong with all this at this point, for most of the time you need to escalate your efforts somewhat in order to determine how severe the problem is. Discussions become focused, formal meetings are arranged, pastors and counselors are brought in. But at some point, *you cross a line*. It is the line between giving time and resources that you can afford to give, and giving what you cannot afford to give. You become depleted, somewhat obsessed, and unable to extricate yourself from the situation. At some point now, it often takes a friend to shake us into awareness and say, *You need to get a life; he's all you talk about nowadays*. Quite likely, he is right.

Ask yourself if you have tunnel vision. Are you focusing exclusively on the craziness of the button-pusher, and not seeing how much of real life you are missing? Is the texture of your thoughts and conversations centered on your relationship? If that is true, begin to re-enter life again. Get involved in whatever was good and meaningful before the problem started. Plug into people who will give warmth and empathy but who will also let you know that they want a more robust relationship with you than problem-solving. Get with them, connect, keep them involved in helping you, but make sure you are involved in helping them and also do some things that have nothing to do with the button-pusher problem. Get your tank full.

Dependency. It is no secret by now that you really do want and desire some good things from your difficult person: love, respect, tenderness, responsibility, affirmation, and the like. There's nothing wrong with wanting something. Desire holds people together and helps them meet each other's needs. But it is a different matter to put a major aspect of your life on hold, waiting for the other person to cooperate so that your life will be better.

For example, a person with a difficult co-worker may find himself thinking all the time about the problem. He will talk to friends and other co-workers about the issue. He will make many different attempts to change things. But he finds that each time his button-pusher acts out again, his day is shot. His life belongs to the person giving him problems. Who is in charge of his happiness? Not himself for sure; the button-pusher is. And the end result isn't a good one. The individual still feels frustrated and powerless, and the difficult person does not change. It is not win-win; it's lose-lose.

The solution is to de-invest, or retrieve, your dependency upon the button-pusher and place it in people who will take care of your needs for you. I am referring to your needs for affirmation, empathy, structure, and reality. When you do that, there are often two very important results. First, the button-pusher begins to miss you, as you are not clinging and intruding on him. It's like the country song, "How Can I Miss You When You Won't Go Away?" There has to be space for the other person to feel longings; resolving dependency provides that space. And second, the button-pusher is more likely to experience his own issues and emptiness. You can avoid your own darkness when you have someone dependent on you. But when that person says, "I'm going to be with some friends; see you," he is more prone to experience his brokenness, selfishness, dependency, lack of structure, or whatever it is he needs to deal with.

Don't be hesitant about admitting you have dependencies. God made us all dependent on each other. Get independent of your button-pusher, and dependent on water from good wells.

Fear of life. It is common also for the person who is in a relationship with a button-pusher to end up defining his life by the problem. It's a little like being an ER doctor, where your entire schedule is dictated by crisis after crisis. However, while the ER physician goes home after his shift, you are on call 24/7. While this may sound draining and unattractive, there is a hidden benefit to it, and it is this: *losing your life to the crisis helps you avoid the risks and anxiety of facing your life.* You may be afraid to go out and find new relationships. Or you may be avoiding feeling the feelings you need to feel. Or it may be scary to restructure your life and schedule so that you are less involved with the button-pusher.

This is a common dilemma among those in relationship with button-pushers. Though their lot is hard, it is easier to live on the defensive with the button-pusher than it is to become a separate and independent person. It is like the parable Jesus taught about the workers who received five talents, two talents, and one talent to invest. The one with the least did not invest his, but hid it in the ground because he was afraid. Not surprisingly, the master was unhappy with him and called him wicked and lazy (Matthew 25:14–30). He was displeased because the worker wasted such valuable resources.

Get some time and space to find out what your talents, passions, and interests are. You may find that you must deal with fears of failure, or new scenarios, or change itself. Face the fears and become a new person. Be in charge of your life, instead of waiting for him to change before you have a life.

As you take control back, you are not being mean or unloving to your button-pusher. In fact, you are doing something very good for him. You are being transformed into someone who can deal with his issue lovingly, in an adult fashion, and not out of fear, need, or desperation. You are preparing to be the best possible redemptive agent for your person and for the relationship.

YOUR GROWTH MAKES A DIFFERENCE TO BOTH OF YOU

Here is some good news about your life as a change agent for your difficult individual: *A growing person is an influence for growth*. This is about getting yourself into the personal and spiritual growth process. Moving into growth actually happens often in a very gradual way: As you work on changing what you are doing with your button-pusher, you are probably growing, maturing, and healing at the same time. They are very interrelated processes. Cheryl changed her style with Kevin, and grew past her anger. Amanda let go of Pam, and grew past her obsessions into moving on.

Think about it this way: What qualifies your button-pusher to be a button-pusher? As we found in chapter 1, it revolves around a lack of ownership. Until that is addressed, nothing of significance happens. One way you can be a force for change in your difficult individual is *to be a person of high ownership yourself.* As you take proper responsibility for your life, you also shift the nature of the relationship toward growth. As you own what you need to, and don't own what is not yours, your button-pusher has less room to blame and deny, and more incentive to change. Don't be afraid to work on your own stuff!

Let's go back to my friend Karen from chapter 3, the one with the mean father. When she started looking at why she was being so wimpy with her dad, she found several things about herself that needed to change. She found that, at the heart of it, she regressed to a little-girl state around her dad (for that matter, around any angry person) and attempted to placate him in order to avoid feeling his wrath, and hoping to gain his love. She didn't understand that for some button-pushers, you can't get their love until you first get their respect. She found that she had such an ideal in her head of a loving, caring dad that she couldn't accept the true dark aspects of his soul. So she tried to forget the crazy dad when he was having a good day. She also understood that she had avoided helping her mom get supportive relationships because she wanted to be the person who was "there" for her mom, and she didn't think Mom needed to need anyone else—a typical idea that kids of fragile parents adopt.

She had a lot of work to do! But it had direction, meaning, and purpose. It was integrated. Dealing with her baggage all pointed to helping Karen be both strong enough and loving enough to more effectively handle Dad and Mom.

Become What You Are Requesting (Modeling)

When you begin to retrieve your life and happiness, and find yourself growing and changing, you are also showing your button-pusher how life should be lived out. You are an example of how love, relationships, responsibility, and freedom all work together for a good result. This can be quite powerful. Remember that your button-pusher is swimming upstream against very strong laws and realities that God designed. This can't be making him happy, unless there are a lot of people rescuing him (don't be one of them!). Yet he is in a relationship with you, and you are abiding by the laws of relationship and doing well. There is something to be said about your life being so full that empty people envy what you have.

Here are some practical ideas to help apply your life and growth to your button-pusher's.

Put down the one-up role. At the same time, stay away from any semblance of one-upmanship, as if you are above your button-pusher because you are happy and independent, or as if you are happy because he is not doing well and you are. That is a dangerous and arrogant position. Remember that you are also broken and unfinished in some way, and need the grace and help of God and others. I have a friend who found God and would go to his friends and tell them, *I can help you now.* They really didn't feel they needed his help, and he had a pretty rough time with them until he became more humble about all that.

Model definition. One of the most powerful aspects of your life that can help your button-pusher is that you become *a defined person.* That is, you need to become clear, honest, and direct about who you are, what you think, and what you want. I have seen so many button-pushing relationships in which the pusher does all the defining, and the other person does all the reacting. For example, the button-pusher gets clingy, then angry, within a couple of hours. So the other person is living totally on the defensive, trying to comfort the dependency and then ward off the anger. This keeps the person who is out of control *in* control—not a good thing.

A defined person isn't easily thrown off balance. He is like an anchor in a storm. He cares, but he does not change who he is. So with the clingy/rageful button-pusher, for example, he keeps an even keel. He is kind toward the clinginess, yet, since he knows it is temporary, he keeps some distance and separateness. He is strict with the rage and either doesn't tolerate it or leaves until it is over; he doesn't try to fix it. This sort of definition provides a structure for the button-pusher to interact with, experience, learn from, and internalize. Often, button-pushers are very unstable inside and need someone who is strong to give them the structure they need.

But What If He Doesn't Change?

That is the million-dollar question. I and many others in the helping fields have seen lots of button-pushers change in long-term and significant ways. Yet, as we have said, people are free, and you have no guarantee that your life will change your button-pusher.

However, think about it this way: There is a huge difference between *desiring someone's growth* and *depending on someone's growth*. When you desire your difficult person to change, you can do it from a position of being loved, strengthened, supported, and being free of his craziness. That doesn't mean you don't feel disappointment in his stuckness or hurtfulness, or that you shouldn't be vigilant to protect yourself from him if need be. But it does mean that your happiness, hope, life, and future aren't focused on someone who shouldn't be running your life.

As the saying goes, pray like it all depends on God, and work like it all depends on you. Though you must hope in God and his process, also work out in your head the possibility that your difficult person may not get the message. Though you may be saddened, you will be saddened from a place of love and comfort. But keep investing in life and good things; keep a full tummy of love and support; and use your modeling to be a beacon of hope to your difficult person.

RESOURCE #3: OTHERS
(SAFE AND SANE RELATIONSHIPS)

ONE OF THE MOST FULFILLING AND FUN THINGS that I like to do is to get people into the process of being in small groups. I have seen miracles of growth occur in them, whether they be support groups, recovery groups, home Bible studies, or therapy groups. There is just something about a small circle, with good people in it who want to go deeper, that cannot be replicated in any other way.

Often, small groups can help make tremendous changes in what is going on with a person who has a button-pusher. People in a crazy-making relationship will sometimes show up in a group thinking that they live on a different planet from everyone else. Their lives of trying to get along with, manage, or adapt to a difficult person seem almost surreal to them, as if they aren't truly alive. Sometimes they may feel like they are pretending, as though they are living externally like a normal person while inside their home or their relationship, things range from frustrating to alienated to bizarre or even destructive. Or they feel like they are a total failure and they haven't done something right, so they have caused this insanity.

I always love it when they start to open up about how crazy their home life, love life, family life, or work life is. They will screw up their courage and hesitantly start talking about some nightmare person that they are in a relationship with. I know they are waiting for someone to say, *Oh my gosh! You are the sickest person in the world to put up with that!* But I also know what invariably happens in good groups is just the opposite. I will see other members leaning toward, and into, the speaker. I will see compassion on their faces. And when it's their time to respond, they will say things like, *I understand. I have a similar situation. I can totally relate. Boy, I'm glad you're in the group; we have some things to talk about.* And I will see the speaker begin to come alive and get safer and more confident that the group will help him deal with this situation.

None of our seven resources to deal with your button-pusher are really optional, and that certainly goes for this third one. Any approach to helping your button-pusher must involve safe and sane relationships; that is, people who care about you, understand, and are on the side of reality. They will help you in many ways to deal effectively with the issue. Good people remove the I'm-the-only-one-in-the-world experience and replace it with *You are not alone; your experience is shared with others.* They provide a sounding board, grounding, direction, and the grace of God for the struggler.

You are guaranteed failure if you do not surround yourself with the right people. That is not meant to sound negative. It is simply the reality that it takes relationship to transform relationship. People who can be around and with you will help you to be the person you need to be to help the button-pusher change. Creating a context for change cannot be done in a vacuum. Get plugged in.

I was counseling a woman whose button-pusher was her brother.

He was not a bad person, but they could not spend any amount of time together before he would become argumentative, provocative, or critical of her.

For example, she would say, "I am going to have to get my car repaired at the dealer's." Her brother would respond, "That's too expensive; go to a shop. You're always wasting your money. I've told you so many times, and you never listen to me." She would try to make her point, but he would just escalate on her. She'd try to smooth things out, but unless she agreed with him on everything, she was in for a lecture.

I worked with her on how he affected her, why she gave him so much power, and how their shared childhood was part of all that. She understood this, but she was also a very isolated person with severe trust issues. So she had no one else in her real life to support her. Consequently, though she had the insight, she could not deal effectively with him.

We began to work on her learning to establish healthy connections with other people that were deep and meaningful. This was difficult work for her, as she was afraid of letting people in. Eventually, however, she got plugged in to some good relationships. These people supported her, let her have her feelings, and gave her good feedback. Basically, they became a second family to her.

When that happened, things began changing with her brother. She was able to confront him when he got out of line. She was more direct about her own requirement for how she wanted to be treated. She even had more empathy for his own struggles. He became more aware of when he was losing it, and their relationship became more mutually beneficial. I do not think the woman could ever have stood up to her brother without her supportive connections.

There are two main areas in which your resource of good people plays a role. The first has to do with your own life and growth, and is general in nature. The second is about people who can help specifically with your button-pushing situation. There is often overlap between the two. The important thing is that all the functions and processes below must be going on, whether it be two different groups of folks, or one group, or some sort of hybrid.

FOR LIFE AND GROWTH

Irrespective of your relationship with the button-pusher, here are several of the most valuable aspects of what relationships provide for you. They are not directly related to the situation, but, make no mistake—if you do not have these relational supports, you are much more likely to fail. It's like how in the world of computers, there is a difference between an operating system and application software. The OS, which is the foundation that makes everything run, has to do with the essential relational components of life presented in this section. Application software involves programs such as word processing and email; those are relationships that are specific to the button-pusher. You can have the coolest software in the world, in the form of experts, mentors, and all the button-pusher's sanest friends. But if you don't have the operating system working, you are simply very likely to fail. Get the OS going first, and plug into relationships for your life and growth.

Acceptance

Acceptance is part of the provision of grace that we all need. Those with a button-pusher often feel guilty, or suffer from a sense that they are failures, or wonder if they aren't good enough or trying hard enough to pull off the required changes. They will often think, *If I loved her enough, she would change.* If this is your experience, you need people who don't require that you have it all together in order to be connected and safe. *To be accepted is to be cared about in your current condition, whatever it is, just as you are:* "Accept one another, then, just as Christ accepted you, in order to bring praise to God" (Romans 15:7).

It is an irony that we often think in order to have relationship and acceptance, we must first have our act together. That is the Law of Moses speaking to us. The reality is that when we are accepted, we then have the choice and freedom to change without fear of losing love. That acceptance derives from the Law of Christ, which is unconditional. There is great comfort in being loved and accepted without having to perform and change. Until you can experience and receive acceptance from people, you cannot truly open up about your doubts, fears, and concerns about your entire life, not just the difficult relationship.

Understanding

This has to do with the ability to enter another person's world, both in empathy and in thoughts. You need people who can "be there" with you. It helps that someone truly "gets" what your experience is like: "The purposes of a man's heart are deep waters, but a man of understanding draws them out" (Proverbs 20:5).

Again, this is not just about your relationship. Remember that the biggest issue is not solving your crazy-making connection; *it is your life and growth.* Never lose sight of that. Your button-pusher may have been the trigger, or catalyst, that got you in touch with your need, hunger, and brokenness, as is often the case. On the other end of things, your growth and health will flow into new ways of being and relating that can greatly help matters.

So don't just look for understanding about the situation. Receive that sort of connection about the entire tapestry of your life. Though no one would minimize the difficulty of the relationship, don't miss the real goods here either. It can be very valuable, especially in terms of seeing how your own past, choices, issues, and hurts tie in to how you have chosen and conducted your difficult relationship. Understanding helps you deal with the situation in a context instead of a vacuum.

Feedback for Growth

Seek truth from people who have taken the time to hear you out and get to know you. Their insights and perceptions will do much to help you. We often have blind spots that can only be noted by someone outside of our skin. Good feedback is balanced with grace and truth so that you can tolerate and metabolize it. Listen to what people say about you: Do they see emotions in your facial expression that you aren't experiencing? Do they note some negative attitude that you should come to terms with? Are there ways of perceiving yourself or others that should be addressed? Ask them to help you grow as a person, and don't resist pondering on any authentic feedback. Use them to help you grow spiritually, personally, emotionally, and relationally.

People, especially in a group context, are a rich source of good feedback because you have several minds observing and reacting to you. Like a second family—the one following the biological family—the group can provide what the first did not, and help repair what damage the first one may have done.

YOUR PERSONAL DELTA FORCE

Now to the specifics. If you have a button-pusher, you are in a conflict, probably many of them. You need particular sorts of things from people who will be your own Special Ops team, to help you navigate how to approach your situation. Here are some of the components to look for.

Normalization

Normalization is the ability to convey a sense to you that you are not aberrant, different, or bad for being with a button-pusher. You may be contributing to her problem in some way, but you are not causing her to behave as she does. You also need to have others normalize that your life is difficult, and that's the way things are.

Sometimes well-meaning friends, or even your own conscience, will tell you that life shouldn't be this way; you must be exaggerating or distorting things. The reality is, it *should* be that way, in the sense that there are good reasons for it. For example, if you live around a controlling person, you should feel resentment toward the controller. And if there are reasons for your dance with the button-pusher, then there can be reasons to extract yourself from the craziness.

Wisdom

Defined as the capacity to live skillfully, wisdom provides the path you need. People with wisdom can direct, guide, correct, and provide insight for you about your situation.

Some people have the wisdom from the school of experience; that is, they have dealt with difficult people in their own lives. They have no illusions about what you are going through. Yet they have learned over time some very valuable lessons. They can give you deeper understanding of your relationship; they can also warn you about pitfalls and things to avoid.

Other people's wisdom comes from formal training or experience; that is, they have studied button-pushers and know what makes them tick and what helps them change. They have seen a great breadth of different sorts of difficult people who don't own their troublemaking, and are well-versed in how to approach things. Good mentors, pastors, counselors, and therapists can be a great help here.

In the past few years, I have seen more and more continuing education courses for psychologists and therapists that focus on how to handle difficult and resistant people, both on a clinical level and on the level of helping family members deal with the person. There is a great deal of information available these days that is well-researched and helpful.

Experiences

Sane people who are on your team can serve as a stage for experience you may need to have. For example, they can role-play with you on what you need to say and do with your button-pusher. They can critique and suggest better ways to do it. Role-playing helps you go through the dress rehearsal without having to do the real thing, so you are more prepared. It is very valuable with button-pushers.

I was speaking at a conference on relationships recently. At one point, I initiated a role-playing exercise and asked for a volunteer to be a particular kind of button-pusher: a defensive, blaming type who didn't want to take responsibility for how much she alienated her family. I took the role of how to handle the situation. The volunteer apparently had had some experience with this type of person. She threw everything in the book at me. Here is a sample:

Me: "Laura, can I talk to you about something?

Laura: "What is it?"

Me: "Well, I've been wanting to go over with you how hard it is to come to some agreement about how you sometimes get overly angry at us in the family, then it seems you think it's our fault."

Laura: "Oh, there you go again. It's always Laura, isn't it? What about the time you got mad at me and hurt my feelings?"

Me: "If I did that, I'm sorry; I wouldn't want to hurt you. Maybe we can talk about that some other time. But to get back to the point, I would like to come up with some solution so that you can hear us when we have a problem with your anger, and make some changes."

Laura: "You're all ganging up on me! Forget you!"

Me: "I don't want you to feel ganged up on. I think we are all for you. But this is a problem, and it won't go away if you walk away. Can you stay and try to work it out?"

Laura: "Only if you understand what you do to me."

Me: "I'll be glad to, but will you agree that after I understand, you'll listen to our side?"

Laura: "OK, I guess."

Laura sat down amidst applause by the audience. She did a great job. I then asked the attendees what their reactions were. One said, *I never knew it was OK to keep getting back on track.* Another said, *I thought being loving meant letting her control the talk.* Others said things like, *I have never seen how to put grace with the truth. I always get mad or give in,* and *I don't think I'll be as rattled next time.* Role-playing walks you through the resistance and gives you confidence and experience.

Reality and Perspective

Most people who care about a button-pusher feel pretty uncertain and disoriented about their own opinions, thoughts, and experiences. It is common for them to be so distracted and outmaneuvered by the defensiveness of the other person that they doubt their own perspective and even adopt the "reality" of the button-pusher. Safe and sane people can go a long ways to re-orient you to what is true, actual, and real.

I often prescribe to people with a difficult individual that they create a "relationship sandwich." That is, when they are going to have a confrontive conversation with the button-pusher (we will go into more detail on this when we look at Resource #5 in chapter 9), they meet with their supportive group and get prayer, encouragement, advice, and love. They go in full of internalized experiences and memories of people who are on their team. Then, soon after the difficult conversation, they meet again, sometimes just a few hours later.

Here they process what happened, especially if their reality was jarred or if they think they were all wrong about this. The difficult conversation is often a regressive experience and causes the person to lose their way. The group steps in and provides reassurance and reality: *You said the right thing. . . . I would tell you if I thought she was right about what she said about you, but I listened to your story, and I think she blamed you for everything. . . . I am proud of you, what a giant step! . . . Hey, you may think she hates you, but we love you. . . . Keep up the good work.*

The safe and sane people rebuild the person's shaky sense of truth and nontruth. It is easy to get hooked into the button-pusher's world and not be able to extricate oneself. Other people are like a lifeline that pulls you back out of the craziness into sanity.

Helping You Hold the Line

There may be times when it is necessary to use limits and consequences with your button-pusher, in addition to your words. We will be dealing with setting and keeping limits in chapter 9. Safe and sane people serve as the protectors and guardians of your own limits. When you are out of strength, or caving in, or feeling guilty, or in danger of not following through with a needed consequence, people can hold you up and strengthen you to hold the hard lines that are designed to bring about change in your button-pusher. This process is a beautiful example of how the Body of Christ is supposed to support the weak member: "Carry each other's burdens, and in this way you will fulfill the law of Christ" (Galatians 6:2).

I once saw this in action with a woman whose husband was having an affair and had left the home. She was turned upside down by this, but got quickly connected in a growth group I was leading. We worked with her on stabilizing things, and getting her values and plans together.

Her husband was stuck in the classic split between the fantasy girl he desired and the stable wife he loved. So when he had an argument with his girlfriend, he would miss the warmth of his wife and want to come over and have relations with her.

She gave in a few times, thinking it would bring them closer. But soon she found that she was only making it easier for him not to commit to anyone but himself. So she began working on saying *No* to him in her group work.

One day she came to group and told us her husband had called and was planning to come over. She missed him terribly, even after what he had done, and wanted to see him. She knew that she was at such a weakened state that she was likely to have sex with him.

The group was terrific. They heard her out, then talked to her about the realities of what she wanted and what giving in would do to her and her plans. I could see her gathering strength as they talked to her. Finally, she told them she was going to cancel the visit. She went home and did that, and came back to group with a victory. It was the first of many tough battles for her. In time, her husband gave up the affair, got help, and eventually came back. She never regretted doing the healthy thing for herself and the kids. The group gave her strength to hold a line that she was not able to keep for herself.

Direct Dealings with the Button-Pusher

There are times when other people can help by being directly involved with the button-pusher, as opposed to being the grounding for the person. This is needed when the situation is extreme or urgent, or simply when the person is in such a weakened or fragile state that she cannot face the difficult person all by herself. And generally speaking, the more the button-pusher respects or identifies with the other people, the more powerful the effects.

Meeting and talking. When the individual is too weak to manage the button-pusher alone, people can simply meet with him and talk to him. They may call on the phone, go out for coffee, or visit him. This has the effect of using other people to drive home the reality that there is a problem. When the button-pusher only hears one person saying there is a problem, it is easier for him to conclude that that sole person is wrong, and he can ignore or overwhelm her. But as more people weigh in with the same perspective, especially people who matter to him, it is harder for him not to listen and pay attention. This is why friends, pastors, and people with some standing in his mind can be of great value.

Also, and this may sound a little simplistic, other people can think of things to say to your button-pusher that you may not have thought of. Their varying experience and perspectives may make an inroad for the lights to come on with your difficult person that has not been done before.

Interventions. In urgent or dangerous situations, sometimes an intervention is necessary. An intervention is an intense meeting with a person who is in denial and out of control in some area, such as substance abuse. Those people who matter to that person, such as his family, friends, co-workers, and neighbors, gather round him and confront him lovingly but very directly about what he is doing to himself and others, and urge him to get help. Interventions correspond to the biblical teachings of bringing others in to talk to an unrepentant person (Matthew 18:15–17). There are people around the country who are formally trained in conducting interventions for various problems, and these processes can be very powerful in breaking through a serious button-pusher's resistances.

I have been involved in interventions, and they can be incredible, though wrenching, times. When you see a person's best friend kneeling before him in his living room, weeping for him and begging him to consider what he is doing to himself and his family, you understand the power of God's love that is distributed through safe and sane people.

Neutralizing. Having other people talk to your button-pusher also has a *neutralizing function.* That is, if the difficult person sees you as the problem, he tends not to hear or respect what you have to say. He may either dismiss or distrust your words. But a third party does not carry the baggage of the dysfunctional history between you two. He is on more neutral ground. This means that he is more likely to respond to the same message that you have been saying, but from the third-party source.

I was consulting with a professional man and his boss once. They were having a problem over how the authority of their relationship was structured. The man thought the boss was controlling, and the boss thought the man couldn't handle authority.

After listening, I sided with the boss and told the man, "I think he's right. He hasn't asked anything of you that wasn't within the purview of the job. Sounds like you are resisting having a boss."

The man thought about it and said, "You know, that makes sense."

The boss was irritated. He said, "That's exactly what I've been saying! How come you can hear it from him?"

"I don't know," said the man. "He just says it in a better way."

I suspected I didn't say it any better than the boss. It's just that, not *being* the boss, I was perceived as neutral.

Pressure over time. Your button-pusher is not likely to make a 180-degree change immediately after a confrontation, though that does happen. There is generally a time element involved, which we will deal with more thoroughly in chapter 11. Your safe relationships can perform a very valuable service by keeping up their presence in the button-pusher's life. In a caring way, they keep the heat up and the pressure on, so that the person knows they won't be going away. He can't wait them out. They need to commit to waiting him out, in a sense. They continue calling, meeting, and visiting. They continue processing the problem with him and inviting him to respond and change. They offer their help and support.

This is not being mean. Rather, it is conveying strength, support, and sometimes protection to the person dealing with him, and, for the button-pusher, conveying the reality that he must deal with more than one person. There is great power in this. If the button-pusher tends to be controlling, for example, he is more likely to restrain himself if the lights of relationship are around him a lot of the time. This sort of pressure can help to melt resistance and secretiveness, and increases the possibilities that the button-pusher will begin to respond. Character patterns tend to get worse in darkness and improve in the light.

How and Where Do I Plug In?

An important thing to consider is who to collect around you as your sane supportive network. There are different levels and types to look at.

"Starbucks relationships." On the most informal level, there are casual connections, or what I call "Starbucks relationships." That

is, these are people you meet with when you can, to catch up with each other. They can help a lot and provide support and encouragement, allowing you to come away from the informal meeting with courage to face another day.

Structured support. However, you will know over time if that is not enough, and the severity of your situation with your button-pusher will let you know whether you need more. I generally recommend to people to go the next step, and that is to some sort of *structured support*. This refers to a small-group type of gathering that meets regularly for purposes of general spiritual or emotional growth. The structure provides stability and reliability of contact, and that is very important, especially if your button-pusher creates chaos in your life. Home growth groups, Bible studies, and small groups are good resources here.

Therapist-led. Then there is a more focused context, which is a group that deals specifically with your type of difficult relationship. This may involve people who are having the same experience, a facilitator-led or a therapist-led group. Here, there is more time and intense energy spent on you and how to address the button-pusher.

One on one. Individual help can be very beneficial too, from pastors who have experience in this world to therapists who are trained to deal professionally with it. At this level, the focus of your time can be dedicated to your situation and ways to resolve it.

On the radio show I co-host, a person with a button-pusher will often call and be at her wit's end. If I think the situation warrants it, I will suggest a couples' therapist.

Many times the caller will say, "But he won't go; I've asked him and he refuses." I will tell her, "Well, I think your situation is serious enough to require a therapist. Put some pressure on him to go."

If she says, "I have, and he just won't," sometimes I will say, "Then tell him that you want him to go to counseling with you. If he doesn't go, you will go to couples' counseling by yourself.

And you and the therapist will talk about ways to deal with him. Wouldn't he want to be part of that conversation?"

Regardless, use the expertise, wisdom, and guidance of an expert.

Get Plugged in Yesterday

So do not go it alone. That is either pride or fear talking, and they are no good for you. Get moving on it now. There is a lot of life to be had in relationships, and God designed you to operate in that way. The right people will help to rebirth life within yourself that you thought had been erased in your struggle with the difficult person. I suppose there is such a thing as too many people involved, as things can escalate or degenerate into gossip or feuds. But generally speaking, the more good people are with you with the button-pusher, the more light shines on the situation. Take the risk, get on the phone, call a friend or a church, and get into a relationship—your third resource.

RESOURCE #4: YOUR STANCE

SCOTT WAS TALKING TO ME about his twenty-two-year-old daughter, Kim. I thought he had good reason to think she was his own designated button-pusher. She was drinking and drugging, in and out of jobs all the time, and moving in and out of the home whenever she was between apartments. Scott was at the end of his rope with Kim. Nothing was working, and she was disrupting his life as well as her own.

I knew the family fairly well and had had the advantage of seeing them interact over the years. So when we started discussing ideas to help, I told him, "She sounds like a handful, Scott, but really, you're contributing to Kim's chaos."

"Contributing? How?"

"Well, let me tell you what I see you do a lot, and let me know if my perceptions are off here," I said. "When Kim seems to be in trouble, you feel sorry for her and give her money and a room. When she makes you mad, you yank it all and threaten to disown her. You have gone into her apartment and raided it for contraband. Another time, you didn't speak to her for months. Then you bailed her out of jail. If I were an unstable and immature person like Kim, I would probably be even more so, with the way you two interact."

Scott thought a minute and said, "OK, so maybe I don't have a good game plan."

I said, "That's probably true, but I don't think that's the real problem. You aren't ready yet for a plan. I don't think you have figured out your basic stance and attitude toward Kim as a person. You're all over the map in your responses to her. You're generous, then you're withdrawing; you feel sorry, then you're controlling, then you're rescuing. So before we talk about any sort of plan, I think you need some basic positions to take with Kim that won't change, and then after that we can start planning."

Scott and I then talked through the principles listed in this chapter and went to work.

POINT OF VIEW

What is a "stance?" Simply put, it is a point of view toward something or someone. It is a broad, guiding attitude that helps direct your decisions, choices, and even emotions toward a person.

For example, when you care about your button-pusher, no matter how frustrated you are about her, you are taking a stance of grace toward her. One of God's stances toward us is a steady, unfailing, and unswerving love: "I will declare that your love stands firm forever" (Psalm 89:2). Especially in a button-pushing relationship when the person is mercurial, moody, impulsive, or unpredictable, you need some basic stances to orient you to how you approach and treat the person. Your stance provides a good measure of structure to the situation and maximizes the odds that the person will respond to your words and actions.

"For" You and Us

The first stance to take is to be "for" her and the relationship; that is, you want the best for her and for you two together. Nothing could be more counterintuitive than this, but it is the best stance to take. You may rightfully and legitimately be very much against her actions, attitudes, and words. However, for you to have the best opportunity to see change and growth, you must be your difficult person's biggest cheerleader. It is the same sort of stance we talked about in chapter 5, about how God is "for" us. It is the stance of grace at its essence—that just as God favors us we are to favor others.

Why is this stance so important? Simply because you are going to be asking, requiring, and setting up structures to influence change in your button-pusher. Change and growth are never easy, even for people who embrace it as a good thing. If you consider yourself a person who is into growth, think about the latest attitude or behavior that you have been trying to change. Even for a growing person, it is work. Then, in contrast, think empathically how difficult change will be for your button-pusher. She has avoided that path for many years, for varying reasons. She has maintained a low ownership of her life and the problems she causes. Her changes have probably been minimal or negative. So it will be quite hard for her to start making the necessary shifts in values and attitudes.

Like a car that has been in a warehouse for years, there is a lot of inertia to deal with when you first turn the engine over. There are rumbles, squeaks, and scrapes as the momentum begins to slowly do away with the inertia. You need to provide lubrication, warmth, time, and patience to help the auto get running again.

No one can successfully execute real change without the grace and support of others to help them along the way. It is just too hard. You are asking your button-pusher to repent, see things your way, listen to feedback, be open to getting help, and a host of other things. She will need the lubrication, warmth, time, and patience that grace and love bring.

The essence of grace is that someone is pulling for your best, invested in you growing and having a good life. That is what grace is all about: It is a stance toward the person that says, in word and deed, *I want your best, and I want us to work out well.*

Agreement? Not Necessarily!

Many times, the person who is in a relationship with a difficult individual sees no value in being on her side. He has tried encouragement, modeling, being positive, and seeing it her way many times, and all of it seemed to have no effect. So he thinks, *She just gets more selfish or out of control when I am nice.* Or, *she thinks I am agreeing with her destructiveness.*

This is a common misunderstanding of having love and grace for someone: the belief that *grace means agreement.* That is, if I am on your side, then I agree that you are right about what you are doing.

Nothing could be further from the truth. Grace has to do with wanting good things for someone; agreement is a value, perspective, and opinion about a subject. Grace is like the ocean, surrounding us and constantly supporting us. Agreement is a specific and finite boat on that ocean. If you don't agree, you change boats to another position, but you stay on the ocean.

Here is a tip: *Be careful not to allow your button-pusher to assume that grace and love equal agreement either.* Often, the difficult person has lived in such a manner that when someone says, *I understand or I empathize,* she interprets it as *I think you are right about this.* Clarify, clarify, clarify. "I want to make sure this is straight between us, Denise: I totally support, accept, and love you; I am for you, and for us as a relationship. But at the same time, your moodiness with the family is a real problem, and I am going to keep working on dealing with it."

Rescue? Doesn't Help!

Not only does grace *not* convey agreement, it does not disburse rescue either. Rescue means to remove someone from having to experience the reality consequences of her behavior. It may mean protecting the irresponsible person from others getting mad at her. Or excusing the chronically angry person so that you don't have to take any action. Or blaming yourself for the Internet porn husband's involvement.

As we saw in chapter 3, when we rescue, we put the weight of the button-pusher's problem on our shoulders rather than on the shoulders of the one who should bear it. Being "for" never means removing someone from reality. Rather, it means *giving someone the love and support required to bear and deal with reality.* It provides the sustenance, courage, emotional presence, and love needed for the person to face what only she can face.

Never confuse grace with rescue; otherwise you run the risk of crossing into license. License is present when grace is given, but it is taken advantage of because the person has no sense of responsibility to use the grace to grow and heal: "What shall we say, then? Shall we go on sinning so that grace may increase? By no means! We died to sin; how can we live in it any longer?" (Romans 6:1–2). The stance to take is, *I am on your side always. But I won't apologize or make excuses for your behavior any more, nor will I make it easy for you to stay the same.*

But I Am All Out of Grace

Grace is not automatically a part of us. A difficult person can exhaust the good feelings and attitudes we need to have toward her.

Years and years and many negative experiences often drain the love you once felt for the person. The resultant thoughts are something like, *I am broken inside about her. Let someone else handle her; I can't generate positive feelings for her any more.*

This is understandable, and it is good to recognize this. You aren't being a bad person when you can no longer feel the outflow of love you once had. It is more a state of emptiness than a mean or selfish state. And there is an answer: *What you do not possess, you must request from the outside.* That is, go to other sources of grace so that you can once again be a dispenser of grace to your button-pusher.

It is absolutely amazing to me how this works. I recently saw a man with a very difficult father simply wash his hands of his dad. It wasn't because he didn't care, but the trauma and craziness siphoned the grace out. But then, when this man got connected to others and received their support, he felt love for his dad rekindling inside. He didn't have to fake it or pretend. He actually was able to give as he had been given to. And his dad has become significantly warmer and softer. I don't think it could have happened without this man seeking out, asking for, and receiving grace and love for himself.

It's Not Fair

All of us tend to deal with this attitude at some point. It just doesn't seem fair to be supportive of the button-pusher at any level. We have done so much, and she has done so little in response. She doesn't deserve it, she doesn't appreciate it, and she is doing nothing for it. *And that is the essence and nature of grace, that God is "for" us when we least deserve it.* He came down to us when we were walking away from him. He did not wait for us to change and repent. He knew we needed an infusion of grace to give us the power and freedom in order to begin changing. Give up the demand for fairness, and be on the side of growth. When you say goodbye to that demand, you end up receiving much, much more.

Your Own Need for Grace

Finally, remember that you need grace for something a great deal more important than having the strength to love your button-pusher: you need it because you are incomplete and in need also. That is the entire human condition, in varying degrees. This has real meaning, because we need to constantly look inside to see all the issues we have. When you are truly honest about who you are, you see more clearly how much it means that God is for you, and what a plight all of us would be in if that were not the case. Those who appreciate that he is on their side can more freely give that grace to others.

YOUR GROWTH WILL SERVE YOUR BUTTON-PUSHER

Related to the "for" stance, but somewhat different, is the stance that your own path of growth should benefit the life of your difficult person. The things you are learning and the changes you are making, as we discussed in chapter 6, should help your button-pusher.

Remember that change and growth are tied in to God's architectural design of how the world works relationally. These principles all work together, and they do not conflict with each other. So as you become more mature and healthier in a process of what the Bible calls sanctification (see Romans 6:19, for instance), your life should promote good things in your button-pusher too. Life brings life; love gives birth to love; responsibility frees others up to be responsible.

As you deal with your own fears, hurts, brokenness, immaturity, sins, or whatever, you should be becoming the most encouraging, loving, fun, humble, honest, responsible, coolest person that your button-pusher has ever seen! He should be saying to himself, *Wow, I've got a good deal here!*

As he receives the benefits of your growth, it can help him become more open to you as a person, and to the process as one that might help him too.

I often see the converse situation, and it is pretty heinous to observe. It goes a little like this: The person gets into growth, driven by how difficult the button-pusher has been. She gets some relief, normalization, and help. Her spiritual life gets better, and she feels hope that she is dealing with issues in herself that need to be addressed.

Then it happens. She enters the world of *growth superiority*, a subtle sickness that affects lots of people. She begins feeling a little above her button-pusher. Her eyes have been opened to life, while he is still blinded. She is on the path to life and growth, while he is lost. She feels closer to God, and he is walking away from God. The sickest part of this is that she will often feel she can no longer relate to her button-pusher because she has come so far, and they are so different now.

That is so not what growth is about, or what the New Testament teaches about growth. The person who is into looking at her issues and changing is certainly grateful for the process, but she is acutely aware of how long a journey she still has ahead of her. She is humble about where she is, and is more concerned about the state of her soul than she is about how lost the button-pusher is. The repentant tax-gatherer's prayer should be her mantra: "God, be merciful to me, the sinner" (Luke 18:13 NASB).

On top of it all, the grower should be able to relate and understand at even deeper levels what the button-pusher's experience is, not less able! If you are growing, your heart and empathic abilities are also. You should be able to enter his world, although you don't agree with it or understand it, although you don't live in it. That is the fruit that growth produces.

Find out what legitimate needs your button-pusher has, what he likes to do, what makes him feel loved, and how you can help him in his own goals. Certainly don't be party to any wrong things or actions that might be harmful to you, but, as much as possible, move toward his life. Don't use your benefits in ways that rescue him from responsibility for his life. But it would be good that he is thinking, *She is different from me, but she doesn't judge or nag, and she is interested in me,* rather than, *I am just a project for her, and she thinks she has arrived.* There may come a time, as we discuss in chapter 10, when you will need to remove some of the advantages of being with you, but if that time is not here, use your growth to serve him.

In practical reality, the person who has that superiority will ultimately negate any influence she may have on her button-pusher. You risk being a party to undoing the changes you have wanted to see. The difficult person will most likely be able to sense this attitude, and who would warm up to someone who feels like you are beneath them? It always concerns me on the radio program when the husband of a "spiritual" wife will call and say, "I feel like I am just the worst person in the world when I am around her." If you are prone to this attitude, read John 13:1–17 and take a class in foot washing! Your growth should be a blessing to the difficult person.

PRESERVING FREEDOM

It is ironic that though your difficult person most likely uses his freedom to cause problems in your life, you must still adopt a stance of preserving and protecting his freedom to make bad choices. He needs to be free to be in denial, selfish, withdrawn, irresponsible, or controlling for there to be any hope that he will make an authentic choice to turn his attitude around.

Were you to force or coerce your button-pusher to treat you differently, he would never make a heartfelt move toward you. Slaves do not obey from the heart; they comply on the outside because they have no power.

It is a lot like the American constitutional freedom-of-speech controversies. One of the founding principles of the United States is that people must be able to be critical of it. That is the only way to insure the freedoms that underlie our structure. Though certainly some people abuse it, it is still an important freedom and must be defended.

This does not mean that your support for your button-pusher's freedom should permit him to hurt you. Take responsibility to protect and guard yourself if he is unsafe with you. However, do not try to manipulate him into doing things differently.

Think of it for a second: If you could force him to be nice to you, that would probably, at first, seem to be an improvement. But how would you feel if you knew the only reason he was being nice was because he was being made to? That would be an empty experience. It is much better to go for the real shift in attitude.

One of my sons recently had a titanic rift with one of his best buddies. As happens at young ages, it blew up, other kids took sides, and they stopped speaking to each other for a while. Barbi and I were sad because we love our son's friend as if he was our own, and we didn't know how permanent the split would be.

We thought about forcing them to make up and be friends, but they wouldn't, and I was OK with that (at least up to a point). I said, "Give them the space to be apart, and see if the missing feelings grow past the mad feelings." I figured there was a lot of good between them, and if they could be free to be apart, the missing would take over. That's pretty much what happened. In their own time, not our adult time, they realized how much they missed the friendship, and that drove them to begin the process of talking and working out the problems.

In some form or fashion, let your button-pusher know, *I want things to change between us, and I need for you to change some things. But you don't have to. You can choose not to. I will not stop you. I may have a response to that, and we can discuss that. I may also protect myself. But I want you to know that you have freedom, and I will not try to control you. If you change, I want it to be because you think it is best.*

You simply cannot lose with this stance.

WILLING TO DEAL WITH CONFLICT FOR GROWTH

This stance has to do with the attitude that the relationship is important enough to you that you will endure conflict and disharmony in order to attempt to make things better. It is the crucible of fire, the risk of experiencing negative things for the sake of growth.

Though it may not seem like it on the outside, this stance has everything to do with love. Love is not about keeping the peace, as sometimes we must fight for peace. Nor is it about maintaining the status quo so that there is no discord. Love is not satisfied with the quiet death of two souls who are externally connected but internally alienated from each other. Love desires and requires that every effort be made for change, growth, and intimacy to occur. If you adopt the stance that you are willing to enter into conflict for the sake of change and growth, you are taking a large step of love.

I was working with Steve and Ann on their marriage. Steve was an intimidating fellow who controlled Ann and the kids by blowing up and being angry when he didn't get his way. She was the peacekeeper type who tried to tiptoe on eggshells around him so he wouldn't get upset. She would calm him down when he had his tantrum by complying with what he wanted. But the next time he was crossed, he would do it again.

I said to Ann, "You're going to have to learn to enter into conflict with Steve."

She said, "But that's so hard, and I don't want him to get even madder."

I said, "Let me show you how well your system is working." I showed her a passage in the book of Proverbs, chapter 19, verse 19: "A hot-tempered man must pay the penalty; if you rescue him, you will have to do it again."

"You're taking responsibility for Steve's temper, and it's getting worse, not better, over time. Something must change. I want you to take a stance for Steve, yourself, and the marriage, and I think the stance should be that you are willing to confront him."

Ann wasn't excited, but she agreed. She did a lot of work to adopt this stance. She dealt with her fears of people's anger. She got support. She role-played conflict resolution. And she began to confront Steve, first in my office, and later at home alone with him.

In my office, Steve did escalate, and I helped her deal with that. He also accused her of not caring about him, which I confronted quickly: "Stop it right now, Steve. Ann is doing a very hard thing by learning to tell you the truth when you're angry. She is trying to help you and preserve the marriage. Get out of your tantrum and listen to your wife, or you are in danger of losing everything."

Steve didn't like any of this, but at heart, he was a good guy. Sometimes, as we said in the last chapter, to have another, more neutral person telling the button-pusher what you have been trying to say, is to help the message get through. He stuck with the counseling and with Ann.

Later, after all this had resolved, Steve was grateful to Ann for being willing to not back down. He said, "I would probably still be running everyone in my life away if you hadn't done that."

Your button-pusher may not rise up and call you blessed for taking this stance. But his perception is not as important as the reality that you are moving in the healthiest ways when you confront for the sake of change and growth.

STANCES DETERMINE PLANS

As my friend Scott was finding out, it's better to get these stances in your head before you plan what to say or do with your button-pusher. They will help you ground your thoughts in the most caring, realistic, and effective way possible. This is especially true if your difficult person has the ability, and you have the vulnerability, to get you off-center and reacting instead of responding. These stances are like setting your sights on a moving target and just waiting for the right moment, not to shoot to kill, but to take action to help.

9

RESOURCE #5: YOUR WORDS

I BROKE ONE OF MY OWN COACHING RULES one day, and realized again why rules exist. I was talking with Nancy, a friend of mine, about her button-pusher mom, Betty. Betty sounded like a handful. Nancy said she was intrusive, dependent, talked too much, and never listened. She would come over and take control of the mood of the home by getting in the middle of things and dominating with endless stories about herself. She was ultimately alienating her adult kids, and even the grandkids didn't like to be around her.

Nancy and I had had several friend-type casual talks about Betty. When she talked to me about the situation, she was free with her anger and her frustration. She was clear and direct about all the things Betty did that annoyed and bugged her: "She goes on and on about trivia, and no one cares!" "I try to get her to ask the kids what they are doing in school, and she starts talking about her own school days." "I'd like to say to her, 'Mom, will you please stop centering it all on yourself and listen to someone else!'"

So when Nancy asked me to ride shotgun on a conversation she wanted to have with her mom, I agreed. She wanted me there for support and clarification. It was a little weird, as I didn't know Betty, and Nancy and I were in a friendship, not a counseling relationship. But I thought, *What the heck, maybe it will help*, and said OK.

The rule I broke, though, was this one: *If you haven't had a confrontive conversation with someone, you first must role-play with a safe person.* Too much can go wrong, especially if you aren't used to confronting, or if the button-pusher tends to be defensive. You need to have faced your stage fright and doubts, as well as the deflections of the other person, in order to push through to the goal of requesting change in your button-pusher. But there wasn't a lot of time before the meeting, and Nancy really didn't think she needed a role-play, so I let it go and we three met.

It was one of the worst confrontive conversations I have ever witnessed in my life.

Poor Nancy. I felt like a judge on *American Idol*, watching a terrible singer perform. I really felt bad for her, because she was working hard, but it did not go well.

First, she never got direct with Betty. Nancy skirted around the issue with affirmations and apologies: "Mom, you know I love you, and I'm so glad we spend time together. I know I haven't always been there for you, and that's going to change."

Affirmation is great, but the point she was affirming to get Betty ready for never got made. She just kept affirming *ad infinitum*.

She didn't listen to Betty. When her mom tried to say something, Nancy went into high anxiety, saying, "I know this is hard for you, and you have been the best mom in the world; you've done so much for us kids." Betty never got a word in edgewise, which for Betty was pretty unusual.

Nancy was clearly too emotional to think or talk straight. Her face was flushed with anxiety; she stammered and spoke too fast so all the words just came out in a pile, with no structure or direction.

Betty left looking a little bemused. I think she was glad she had met a nice friend of Nancy's; that was about all that in her mind had happened. As I debriefed the debacle with Nancy, I said, "So what do you think happened?"

"I just froze up. I couldn't say what I wanted to say," she said.

I said, "You know, when we talked before, you were very clear with me about what you wanted to say."

Nancy said, "Yeah . . . I suppose talking *about* Mom is different from talking *to* Mom."

I couldn't have agreed more. And I apologized to Nancy for not insisting on role-playing beforehand. I have never made that mistake since.

Your Words Are Important in Changing Things

I hope I did not discourage you with Nancy's story. Its intent was to convey a couple of points: first, that you probably need to have a conversation with your button-pusher; and second, that you probably need to know how to do it in the best way possible. There is a good way to do it, and we will unpack the elements of that in this chapter.

Though it can certainly be an uncomfortable process, your button-pusher most likely needs to hear your words in order to change. That is just the nature of relationships. One of our grand tasks with one another is to confront, give feedback, ask for change, and so forth, even as we are "speaking the truth in love" (Ephesians 4:15).

Words have meaning and provide information and direction. Even the most relationally attuned non-button-pusher needs to hear from those in his support system so that he will benefit from their perspective, insight, and truth.

Don't make the mistake of trusting that your changed life, your love, and your modeling are enough. Your difficult person can interpret that as being a sign that you are happy with the way things are, and that you have no issues to bring up.

There are several aspects to having a talk with your button-pusher about what you want to see changed. As you look at these, see which ones you already have ability and skill on, and which ones may need some work.

TONE AND CONTENT

Every conversation has two dimensions to it: *tone* and *content*. Tone has to do with how your voice sounds when you say something, and content is what you are saying.

Tone

Tone is highly important, as you can negate the words you are saying with the way you sound. We have two Labrador Retrievers in our family. The other day, the kids and I were playing with them in the backyard, and one of my sons said, "Watch this." He went to the dogs and said, in a cheerful, friendly voice, "You dogs are pretty useless; we don't want you around any more, do we now?" The dogs scurried and hopped around him like he was praising them to high heaven. Then he said, in a gruff, angry voice, "Good doggies, sweet doggies." They looked quizzically at him and moved back a step or two. Then, to reassure them, we immediately praised the dogs again and played with them so they would know things were OK. That's an example of how your tone matters, and will matter, in a confrontive conversation.

It makes sense. You can pretty much assume that when you tell your button-pusher that you would like to meet and talk, she will be aware that you think there is a problem. The very act of asking for a meeting—and I do believe that you should, as opposed to doing this on the fly—conveys import and seriousness. So her guard is likely to be up. She may already be anticipating that you don't like something about her, and she may know already what you want to talk about. So the tone you begin and conduct the conversation with must serve the purpose of conveying the first stance that we discussed in chapter 8: you are for her and the relationship.

The best tone to have is one that is warm. Warmth conveys safety and care, and that stands the best chance of keeping your button-pusher from becoming even more wary or defensive than she already is. You can convey warmth even when you disagree, and you need to learn that ability. Now, you may be angry or afraid of your button-pusher, and can't feel a lot of warmth for her because of what she has done to you. If so, go elsewhere first, and confess and process those feelings. Don't bring them in, as you run the risk of escalating things and not getting the results you desire. Remember that in a sandbox fight, there needs to be an adult present to keep some safety and order. If you can't be the grownup, don't depend on the button-pusher to be either. Get into the adult role, then call for the talk.

Speak from experience. When you talk to your button-pusher, speak from your experience and life. Talk from the heart. Use "I" statements as much as possible. Stay with what you feel, think, and perceive.

There is a tendency we have to speak "at" the person, to use all-or-nothing language, and to speak *ex cathedra*, as if our reality is the final authority. These can cause formidable obstacles to your person's willingness to hear what you want him to change. Read these two statements to see the contrast:

You are angry with me all the time, and you need to stop.

It seems to me that you are angry with me pretty often, and it is difficult for me to be close to you.

In the first statement, there is little vulnerability. In the second, she lets him know she wants to be close but can't. In the first statement, her reality is fact: he is too angry. In the second, it seems that way to her (it's possible that she has a sensitivity to anger and over-reacts to normal anger). In the first statement, it's all the time. In the second, it is often. Learn to talk from your gut and your experience; it helps bring walls down in your difficult person.

Content

The next elements have to do more with the content of what you want to say. They are in a general chronological order, but there is some play and room here. Be flexible, according to how things are going.

Affirm the good. It is probably best to begin the talk with taking the initiative to affirm, or validate the reality of, what is good in your button-pusher and in the relationship itself.

An affirmation can be simply a recitation from you of some of the things you like, appreciate, and want to see more of in him. This is particularly important, as many difficult people do not perceive confrontation as being loving, helpful, or "for" them in any way, shape, or form. Their experience with confrontation may be from an abusive parent. Or they may never have received confrontation from anyone, so they have no skills to understand or use it. So, because of their own inexperience with the values and blessings of feedback and their conclusions about their own "rightness," they tend to identify confrontation as hatred, persecution, or condemnation. That is why, when you affirm, you make it easier for them to feel safe and able to metabolize what you want to say later. They can listen from a loved position rather than from a guarded one.

You might start with some things like this:

"Thanks for meeting with me. I wouldn't have asked you to take the time unless I thought it was important, and I want you to know that you are important to me. This isn't about putting you down or criticizing you. I am in this relationship with you, and I am here for the long run. I am on your side, and our side. I love you, and I want things to be good for you and for us.

"I know we are having some rough times, but I want them to be better. There are a lot of great things between us that I want to keep and develop. The good times are really the best, when we are having them. I really believe God has put us together, and he wants us to be connected. You have so many good points, like your work ethic, your parenting, how your friends love you, and how good you are to me when things are going right.

"So all I want to do in this conversation is to talk about a problem in order for us to solve it. I want to get it out of the way and out of our lives because it comes between us, and it hurts the relationship, and it hurts me. I want it resolved, because I want to get on with a good life and closeness with you. Does that make sense?"

This question is a real question. It is designed to make sure that he gets it that you affirm him, don't want to blast him, and just want to get a problem resolved so that you can reestablish closeness again. He may project his own anger or guilt into what you said, like "You're saying that I'm the bad guy." If he does, clarify it: "No, no, that's not what I'm saying at all. I'm saying that I love you and I want to be close to you again, and this problem is like a boulder in the middle of the road. I just want the boulder out of the way, because *I want you*. Does that make sense?"

Most of the time, in time, this conveys the safety you want to bring, and you can go to the next part. If, however, your button-pusher persists in perceiving that you are coming down on him, keep trying, sometimes in a different talk session. But if it never gets there, you may need to bring in a neutral third party to help. You just can't get to the point until he first understands the affirmation.

It will not be safe enough for him to attend in any constructive way.

Hear him out. It sounds ironic, but the conversation stands a better chance of you making your point if you will, early in the talk, *shut up and listen!* I am not trying to sound unkind, but the reason for this is that everyone has their own point of view already running around in their heads. Think about the last time someone confronted you about an issue. Unless you are a very good and non-defensive listener, you were probably forming the words to respond to them *while they were still talking*. You probably weren't really attending to every nuance they were saying. So it is likely that your responsive words had more to do with your internal conversation than addressing the concern of the person confronting you.

Now, think empathically about the button-pusher for a minute. He is likely to do a lot of self-justifying, blaming, and excusing anyway; that is part of his ownership problem. So this trait compounds the tendency to not listen to a confrontation, block the person out, and start forming an excuse or a counterattack. All the more reason to hear him out first.

Hearing out your button-pusher at the beginning of the conversation helps to clear out his internal conversation so that there is more room and space in his mind for your words. It helps him feel that you care about his point of view and are not just there to blast him. And it is just the right thing to do. Everyone needs his day in court, his time to protest or show his side of things.

On a strategic and wisdom note, hearing him out may be valuable to your agenda for change. You may hear something in his point of view that might illuminate or inform you, and you can know better in what direction to take things. I don't mean this to sound manipulative, but the last person to show his cards tends to be in more control. Hold your tongue and hear him out.

So don't go into your entire message about the problem yet.

Touch on it to give him context, but begin instead with something like this:

"I wanted to talk to you about our relationship, especially my experience of you as being too angry with me. But I really want to first understand your side of things. Can you tell me what it's like for you, if you see this the same way, or if I'm doing something here that isn't helping?"

Now wait. Except in very rare cases, your button-pusher should feel the grace and permission you are extending and present his side of things. He may not be organized or warm. He may be angry, which you need to contain and listen to, to a point. If, however, he gets too heated and it isn't subsiding, you may need to say, "I know this is getting pretty emotional for both of us; can we postpone this for a bit when we feel better?"

Listen empathically. Do not make the mistake of correcting his perception of you here. That does not further your mission; in fact, it can lose ground for you. Be still and understand his opinion. You are not agreeing; you are listening. And, if he has some valid points about your contribution to the problem, agree, apologize, and let him know you will change. Say something like this: "I think you are right, that I nag and don't let go of things with you. I can see how that makes matters worse. I'm sorry for that, and I will work on that."

However, *don't hear him out forever*. Some button-pushers get into their own protest, and it can take on a life of its own. Their internal world is filled with themselves as the victim and others as constantly not treating them well. They can go round and round with this, with no resolution. They simply don't have the structure to stop it. So, when you think you have "gotten it," at least the basics, and he hasn't wound down, say something like this:

"OK, I think I get your end of it, at least what is primary: You do get angry and withdrawn sometimes, because the job is hard, but you think that I am overreacting and it's not as bad as I say. And I make things worse when I nag and don't get off your back. Do I have the general gist of it?"

If he says you don't get it, then go through the process again until both of you agree, *not on the reality,* but on the button-pusher's perception. If you find this isn't working, get some training in listening skills from someone. Learning to paraphrase another's experience is a well-known and valuable tool to have.

Also, be aware of any tendencies you might have during the hearing-out phase to resent that he gets to be understood, and not you. This isn't about playing fair, or even mutuality at this point. You are intentionally delaying some of your own desires for a higher purpose, and that is increasing the odds that he will attend to your requests for change. Don't cut off your nose to spite your face. Extend, hear, give grace, and wait.

State the problem. Make it direct and simple. Don't beat around the bush like Nancy did, but don't be unloving either. It is about clarity and simplicity so that he can understand it as well as possible. You want to state what it is your person is doing and how it affects you and others.

The Level of the Problem: Begin with What is Observable

Frame the problem in terms of what can be seen, observed, even measured. Tell him about specific behaviors or words that illustrate the problem: "You get overly angry at home. You yelled at me last night when I asked why you were late to dinner." This lessens the chances of him denying or questioning that these things happen.

What is observable generally has a root cause to it. In this instance, for example, maybe the husband feels powerless and uses anger to regain a sense of control; or he is so isolated that he can't soothe himself in stressful situations, so he blows up. *Whatever the cause, it is of secondary importance at this point.* Your focus is to tell him what is, not why it is. Certainly, were he to admit what he does and then be curious as to why you think he does it, you should go into it. But stay with the behavior.

State the problem's effect. It wouldn't be a problem to you if it didn't affect you in some negative way. Present the problem *in terms of the relationship as much as possible.* The more you show how what he does hurts the "we," the better your chances of breaking through his defenses and resistances.

Here's an example:

"Your yelling scares me and the kids too. They woke up last night. And I really distance from you when you do it. It is very hard for me to get close to you with that level of anger. It just shuts me down inside, and I can't get past it, even though I want to. I miss being close to you, but it is too impossible when you are that mad. Then, when you aren't angry any more and want to be close, my feelings haven't changed and I stay away from you."

You are trying here to elicit empathy and compassion from him regarding how his behavior is hurting people he loves and relationships he values. If he cares for you and others, that can be effective. If, however, he is too self-absorbed, afraid, or uncaring to be moved, don't give up. It just may mean other parts of this section will have to come into play.

For example, you may have to say, "So you admit you get irrationally angry and scared and distance me and the kids. But you also seem to be saying that you don't care. Are you saying that?" Sometimes, having to own a statement like that will help a button-pusher to begin to see what he is doing. Not many people would like to identify themselves as someone who is doing something hurtful, and not caring who it hurts.

Attitudes. Sometimes a button-pusher doesn't manifest behaviors or words. His craziness comes out in attitudes, which are more difficult to pin down. For example, he may have a condescending or contemptuous tone. He may be maddeningly polite, but be cold and unavailable underneath. He may have a subtle shift of mood when you disagree with him, which lets you know he is angry, but it isn't said.

He may not even be aware himself of these attitudes. However, state them from your experience:

"When I talk to you about my day, you answer me but it sounds mechanical, like you are thinking about something else. I don't know another way to describe it, except that you seem preoccupied with your thoughts and dismissive of mine."

If he admits them, you are on the way. But if he does not, say, "How about if I mention it the next few times I experience it, so you can see what I mean?" Bringing up an attitude in the now can help. If he still does not get it, and you have tried several times, you may have to resort to help or consequences, as we go into in chapter 10.

OWN YOUR STUFF

Your button-pusher needs to know that you are not playing the superiority game with him, as we discussed in the last chapter. He is less likely to want to be open to you if he thinks you see yourself as the morally superior force who is trying to help the wretch. That is why you need to sincerely own and take responsibility for what you have done to make things worse, either by omission or commission.

As we illustrated in the previous part, this may happen when your person is presenting his side of the matter. However, there may be more to what you need to own, which your difficult person has not mentioned. If he has not brought those issues up, but you know they exist, take initiative to talk about them.

A good place to begin, before the conversation, is to review chapter 3 and identify problems you can relate to having caused or contributed to. Then, during the talk, bring them up and deal with them:

"As I think about it, I have realized that I have made things worse for you and us. I have done a lot of threatening without following up on threats. Like the time I told you if you yelled again I would leave. I didn't do it. It was wrong for me to say one thing and do another. I should have either left so that you wouldn't have gotten a mixed message from me, or I should have come up with another consequence that I would have followed through on. I can see how I confused things.

"Also, I have not spoken up when you have hurt me, and I have just gotten quiet and resented you. I think that has made it hard for you to know when your anger crosses the line, because I don't speak up. And my resentment has been pretty judgmental. I have just stewed and condemned you in my mind. So I want you to know that I am aware of these things. I am sorry for them, and I want to do my best to change. I want you to let me know if you experience me doing them, and I will listen to you."

Fairness Again

This is an FYI. As you own, apologize, and repent to your button-pusher, you may again notice feelings of *This is not fair—I am having to humble myself, and he is the real problem*.

Yes, you are having to humble yourself. However, humility is the best place in the world to live. It is where God and reality are. And no, your button-pusher is not the "real" problem. Though you may be a minor contributor and he a major one, your issues are just as real as his are. Embrace humility and change because it's good for you and your life. Don't keep score.

A good friend of mine once had a conflict with a co-worker.

Finally, he went to the co-worker and apologized. My friend was really bugged when the co-worker accepted his apology but didn't apologize back. That wasn't in the script in my friend's head. He almost took his apology back! I said to him, "You need to question the sincerity of your apology, if you required that of him." He thought through it and realized he had gotten into the fairness "tit for tat" thinking. Eventually, my friend was able to let it go and get along with the co-worker without the demand for equal apologies.

REQUESTING CHANGE

Having done all of the above processes, say what you want him to change. Don't be afraid to say "you" here, unless it is entirely a "we" thing such as, "I want us to stop being so busy that we don't have time for each other." In most cases, even if there is a "we," it is more helpful for definition and clarity of responsibility to parse out the "you" and the "I" from the "we."

Basically, it comes down to the reality that you want him to stop a bad thing, or to do a good thing that he is neglecting. Keep it at that level for now so that it does not get complicated. One of the take-aways you will want in the talk is for him to not misunderstand what you are requesting. You don't know when you will find another opportunity to talk, and he could be much more defensive the second time.

Here are some examples:

"I want you to stop being so angry with me."

"If you are angry, let me know what is wrong in a calm way so we can talk about it."

"If you are really mad at me, go take a walk or call someone before you bring it to me, so that you are calmer about it."

"I want you to talk to me about your anger and admit that you are angry before you start blaming me and yelling. That way we can deal with your anger together."

There is no one way to do this; use what fits you and the situation the best. But speak from what you want and need.

Stuck in a Confrontation Cycle

Sometimes, the person has been so fed up for so long with the button-pusher's behaviors that she gets stuck in a confrontation cycle. It is as if she has been in prison, and now she finally gets to say what she feels. This can be a problem, as she goes on and on about what the difficult person has been doing and never gets to what she wants. There is certainly a time for your protest and complaint to be heard, but this is not the time.

I worked with a couple once where this happened a lot. She said, "You stay withdrawn and isolated; you don't help with the kids." He said, "What do you want me to do?" She said, "You watch TV, and you aren't available." He said, "OK, what do you want me to do?" She said, "It's like you aren't there . . ."

I finally had to interrupt and say to her, "Unless you answer his question, I am going to tell him not to pay attention until you tell him what you want." She understood, and that helped her break out of the cycle.

Requesting beyond Choice

There are those times in which what you desire is something that is beyond the difficult person's choice. For example, a substance abuser may not be able to stop. A chronically depressed person may not be able to choose to be happy. In fact, using the example we are dealing with in this chapter, the angry husband may, when he tries to stop, find that the anger problem is beyond him.

Pay attention ahead of time to that possibility. You don't want to get in the problem of asking something that the person can't do, even if he wants to. Instead, if this is the case, *request something he can do that will help empower him to change*. There is always a next step, even if it is the first step in a process of change. Tell the substance abuser you want him to get into treatment now. Tell the depressed person you want him to call a therapist this week. If the angry husband has a history of sincerely trying to control his anger and keeps failing, tell him you want him to talk to someone who knows about these matters (such as a group, expert, pastor, counselor, wise friend) this week.

It may be that at this point you don't know what is beyond choice and what is not; he may have never admitted he has a problem yet. If that is so, getting admission and a commitment to stop the bad behavior is probably enough. Then, if you find that he is trying and failing, it is a deeper problem than you thought, and it is time to get some resources to assist him.

Deal with Deflection

Be prepared for the possibility that, though you have gone through the steps of the talk, your button-pusher may still be resistant. He may deny, minimize, rationalize, or blame the problem on you. Don't be surprised by this. Understand that many button-pushers have used deflection of responsibility as a life pattern for a long time. Accepting responsibility for bad behavior is something that he may be avoiding at all costs. Remember that for you this may be a quest for truth, but for him it may be a way to get out of pain and blame.

Though it might be a setback for you, stay in the game. This is not a time to fold, quit, become passive, blow up, or decide to leave the relationship. It is a signal that *you have a second problem to deal with besides the issue you are bringing up*. There are approaches you can utilize to help get through his deflections of your message.

Listen, Then Get Back on Track

Hear out the excuse or blame, but refocus on your request for change:

"I understand that you think you wouldn't be angry if it weren't for me. And I'd like to talk about that sometime, maybe tomorrow night. But I want to get back to my request for you to not be so angry at me when you get home."

That isn't being controlling of him. Instead, it's being in control of yourself and your part of the conversation.

Remember that during the hearing and owning parts of the talk, you already did listen, consider, own, and apologize for whatever you have done. So open season on you is over until another time. Don't get lost in endless cycles of blame. There is a time and place for that, but not now.

Shift the Focus to the Resistance

If, however, after several attempts at reasoning, your difficult person keeps wiggling out of admitting what he is doing and shows no signs of progress, you will want to stop trying to get back to the problem and now *make the resistance the problem*. That is, if you are still arguing, convincing, chasing him down, and interminably refocusing, this is a sign that your button-pusher's lack of ownership is really what is keeping the problem going.

Now you are dropping to a deeper level, and it can be very helpful for both of you, as it probably lies at the core of the biggest issue of the relationship anyway. Say something like this:

"I'm feeling pretty helpless right now. Every time I attempt to show you that your anger is a problem for me, you either blame me, tell me I'm overreacting, make excuses for it, or get angrier. This isn't being productive for either of us. I'm becoming aware that no matter whether it's anger, or parenting, or money, or sex, *I can't talk about problems with you in a way that solves them for us*. So a lot of our issues don't ever get resolved. I can't imagine that this is pleasant for you either. Can we work on that as a problem?"

Another tack you might take is to transfer responsibility for receiving feedback on him. Since he avoids hearing your reality, stop trying to "say it the right way," which is a common mistake people make. You aren't a mind reader. Instead say, "When I confront you or give you feedback, it doesn't go well. You feel like I am being unfair, or don't understand you, or I am being mean. I don't want you to feel that way, because I'm not any of those things. Here is what I would like: *I want you to tell me how to tell you the truth, in a way that you can feel OK about hearing it.*"

Make him part of the solution; it's his mind and ears that are involved. He may say, *Reassure me that you still like me*, or *Give me a minute to cool down*, or *Give me a positive affirmation*, or *Give me a heads-up that it's coming*, or *Tell me when it's a better time*. Consider what he says, and if it is reasonable, do it that way. If he is receptive, you are making progress. If not, continue making the resistance an issue.

LEARN TO WARN

Having a talk like this with your button-pusher has more than one purpose. It should attempt to reestablish connection and communication, solve the problem, and get you on the same page with some solutions. But there is another purpose: *the talk is also diagnostic of the character of your difficult person.*

A person who can ultimately be touched with your vulnerability, ownership, love, and reality is a person who probably doesn't need much more pressure, except to stay in the process of change. But a person who refuses, directly or indirectly, to see or admit that what he is doing is destructive or hurtful is telling you that he may require not just words, but actions.

The Bible teaches that if several people go to a person with a problem, and he doesn't listen to them, then they are to move to consequences and limits (Matthew 18:15–17; 1 Corinthians 5:1–5). This is not being unkind. It is more that you must respond to the level at which the button-pusher may more readily respond. Some people respond to the hurt they cause others. Others require some sort of pain in order to learn that it will cost them to keep hurting others. They are more motivated by the pain-pleasure principle than by empathy. It is a lower level of responsiveness, but working at that level can be very effective for people who do not listen to verbal entreaties.

We will deal more thoroughly with limits and consequences in chapter 10. But before you set limits, you need to warn the person that they may be coming. Giving a warning can, in and of itself, help change behavior. A person may become aware that you are so serious about the problem that you are willing to entertain a consequence. That is progress.

Often, however, the person may see the warning as meaningless and not respond. In that case, be prepared to act, as we will discuss in the next chapter.

Timing

It is probably best not to go into warning until you have tried a few times to work it out by talking. Sometimes the repetition and persistence help. Also, as the Bible teaches, you may want to bring about other people to assist the process before warning, as we discussed in chapter 7. Tell him you want to go together to talk to someone. That is not really a consequence, as there is no discipline involved. It is more a relational move. Unless it is urgent, dangerous, or life-threatening, try confronting several times. The button-pusher may simply not be used to you confronting him, at least in this manner.

However, if all else is failing, warn of the coming result. For example, you might say, "You aren't listening or admitting that your anger is a real and serious problem. I am not going to keep talking to you about this. But I want to let you know that I am not going to tolerate it either, even if you do insist that you aren't doing it. The next time you raise your voice at me in an angry manner, I will leave the house and go to Nicole's for a while. And if you continue it, I will take further actions until you have taken steps to stop."

When you are warning, be firm, strong, and direct. You do not want there to be any mistaking what you are saying. If you don't mean it, or don't think you can follow through, don't say it. Work on being strengthened in your safe and sane relationships, and then warn when you are prepared.

Remember that God has been warning us, and telling us to warn each other, for ages (Ezekiel 3, 33). It is a gift and a blessing to give someone a chance to change by warning. Don't look at it as a bad thing, but a necessary thing. It may be the thing that begins to turn life around for your button-pushing relationship.

AS YOU CAN PROBABLY TELL, the talk will take some preparation, prayer, and role-playing. It is better to be overprepared than under-prepared here. Spend the time on being able to conduct the talk. You will know the next steps by your person's level of responsiveness. Again, supposing the response is not what you would desire, then it is time for the actions prescribed in the next chapter.[1]

RESOURCE #6: YOUR ACTIONS

TOM SAT ACROSS FROM ME AT THE RESTAURANT. He was quiet, but I knew what he was thinking. He was getting ready to cross a line that he had never crossed before. I waited. Finally he said, "Yeah, I'm going to call her today."

"Call me after you talk," I said.

The "her" Tom was talking about was his mother, Andrea. Without going into the details, she had been a pretty poor mom during his childhood. Andrea had had a lot of dependency, immaturity, and divisiveness that had caused him a lot of trouble growing up. However, Tom had gotten good help, support, and counseling during his adult life, and he really had dealt with his baggage from her. He forgave her and went on with his life. Andrea was still the sort of person she always had been, and would blame him for things out of the blue sometimes, but he chalked it up to her issues and didn't take it too seriously. He had a good balance about his mom. He didn't expect a lot from her, and, though he was friendly with her, he didn't spend a lot of time with her either. From time to time, he, his wife, Chris, and their son, Matt, would visit her or have her over to their home.

The problem at hand, however, did not now revolve around Andrea and Tom, but around Andrea and Matt. She wasn't a great grandmother either, but she had been OK until now. In the last few weeks, however, when she was angry at Tom for some real or imagined slight, she had changed tactics in a very destructive manner. She had begun to call Matt, who was now about thirteen, when she could get him on the phone away from his parents. She would tell him negative and untrue things about Tom in order to get back at her son. It was a vengeful and sick thing to do. She was clearly a very disturbed button-pusher.

Understandably, this upset the boy a great deal. He told his dad and mom about it, and he was torn up inside to have his own grandmother trying to turn him against his dad. It was a traumatic experience for Matt. Tom acted quickly. He called Andrea and told her that she was not to call Matt directly again, but to go through him from now on. He warned her that she was jeopardizing her relationship with all of them if she did not stop. But it did not end there. A few days later, Andrea again called Matt when Tom and Chris weren't around and criticized him for "telling on her" to Tom. Tom became very upset and angry at how destructive Andrea was being to her own grandson. He recognized the repetition of how she had been in his childhood. Again, he called her and told her to stop. And again, she ignored him and called Matt behind their backs. Tom had instructed Matt to not answer the phone anymore, but with a teenager, that one was a little unreasonable and unenforceable.

Tom told me that it was time to go beyond words to actions with Andrea, and I agreed with him. That day, he called her and said, "Mom, I wanted you to know that I think at this stage you are toxic with our family. You have hurt us, and continued to hurt us, and you have not listened to my requests to change. So from now on, we will not have any contact with you until you apologize and ask forgiveness for what you have done to me, to Chris, and to Matt individually."

From what Tom told me about that conversation, it was a brutal one. Andrea yelled, cried, and accused him of being mean and judgmental. She refused to even consider what he had asked, and hung up on him. If that weren't hard enough, she began calling them up, but not to apologize. She would start blaming and playing the victim. She called Tom's sister and brother and convinced them that Tom was being cruel to her.

But Tom, Chris, and Matt did not move from their stance. When she called, they would say, "If this isn't about apologizing, I'm going to hang up now." She would scream or cry, and they would hang up. This happened several times, and then Andrea wrote them a letter saying that she herself was cutting off all contact with them, because they were being so mean.

Tom went through a lot of mental and emotional turmoil during this time. He often doubted himself. His conscience attacked him about how unforgiving he was being. (Not true: Forgiveness is about yesterday, which Tom had dealt with; he was protecting tomorrow.) Even a few of his friends thought he was being too harsh. Matt missed his grandmother, though he knew she was very difficult. Tom even experienced some emotional regressions relating to his own childhood, which is common in these sorts of situations. But he stuck to his convictions and his limits.

Two years passed. Then he got a call from Andrea. When he picked up the phone, she said, "I'm sorry for what I did. Will you forgive me?" And she was serious. He was blown away. His mom, who was virtually dead to him, had come alive again. He said of course, and she then talked to Chris and Matt, and reconciled with them too.

Very happy, but also cautious and curious, Tom asked Andrea what had happened. She told him that basically it had taken that long a time, and the help of some friends, to realize that she was wrong, and how much she missed them. That was what it took to humble herself enough to ask forgiveness for her hurtfulness. Tom understood and, in time, began re-establishing visits and phone calls with Andrea. To the date of this writing, it has been several months now and things have remained good enough to continue. As Tom says, "Andrea is still Andrea, but she doesn't do anything really serious anymore, so it's OK."

The line Tom crossed was the line from words to actions. He tried talking, several times, and finally decided he had to set some limits, if not to help Andrea get better, at least to protect his family. Obviously, it was a very difficult move. But, had he not done it and stayed with it, I doubt that Andrea would have made the changes that she did. Sometimes it takes actions to give weight to your words.

The Power of Actions

Your actions are your sixth resource. The right kind of behaviors and moves on your part, handled in the correct manner, can have tremendous power with your button-pusher. They support what you are saying. Many difficult people just do not listen to, believe, or respond to what others say to them. In their experience, most people either confront, nag, or threaten, but there is no meaning past the words. The reality is that many button-pushers simply require some sort of painful experiences in order to learn that people mean what they say. An ancient proverb says this is the difference between a person of understanding and a foolish individual: "A rebuke goes deeper into one who has understanding than a hundred blows into a fool" (Proverbs 17:10 NASB).

Using action has nothing to do with revenge or anger. In fact, taking the appropriate steps and consequences is often the cure for one's own anger as you regain control of your life and make moves toward helping your button-pusher. The motive to keep in mind, as with all the resources, is love: you are for the person, his growth, and the relationship.

Let's evaluate the primary action terms in respect to the story of Tom and Andrea. To briefly define things, a *limit, or boundary, is a line you draw which defines things.* It can define who you are and who you are not; for example, *I am for us both having freedom in this relationship, and I am against one of us controlling the other.* It can define that which is your responsibility, and that which is not; for example, *I care about you, but I can't take responsibility for your emotions.* It can define what you will tolerate and what you will not; for example, *I will put up with some irresponsibility in you, but I won't put up with your working so much that you neglect the kids.*

When you set a limit with your button-pusher, you are drawing a line for both of you, which informs him that you will not accept behaviors past a certain point. It is your request and your rule. In Tom's case, his initial boundary with his mother was that she was to go to him first when she wanted to talk to Matt. He was saying to Andrea, "I am taking responsibility for my family's welfare. I am not taking responsibility for keeping you happy, if you require treating us that way to be happy. And I am letting you know what I will not put up with."

Then, as we saw in chapter 9, a *warning* serves notice to the person who ignores the boundary request. It conveys that if this continues, something will happen which will be unpleasant to the person who violates the limit and crosses the line. Tom gave notice, so to speak, to Andrea that her relationship with his family was at risk.

A *consequence* is different in concept from a boundary. Technically, a consequence is the *result of a boundary violation*. It is an action that you perform if the person crosses the limit you have set. Consequences serve to *back up and enforce boundaries*.

As we mentioned earlier, a consequence is either the presence of something undesirable or the absence of something desirable to the difficult person. So when Andrea violated Tom's limit, the consequence was a loss of contact with them. Gauging from her reaction, this was a very painful loss for her. It was not intended to harm Andrea. Instead, it had the dual purpose of protecting the family from her divisiveness and of bringing home to her the reality that her attitudes were associated with results. She was not free to do or say anything she pleased without a consequence. That is true of us all. It is a major rule of life and relationship. And, in this case, though it took quite a long time, it helped Andrea face her responsibility for her behaviors. *Consequences are not everything you need to deal with your button-pusher, but they are central*, especially when there is a lot of violation going on.

So the concept of boundaries, warnings, and consequences is fairly straightforward and simple. You see it all the time in parenting, for example. Mom tells six-year-old Danny to pick up his clothes from the floor (boundary). When he ignores her, she tells him that there will be a consequence if he doesn't do it now (warning). When he continues to go his own way, she confiscates the same toys he has been using to dawdle for some period of time, while still requiring him to pick up the clothes. And hopefully Danny begins to symbolize and *internalize* (to internalize is to take these emotional experiences inside himself and make them part of his inner world and reality) the boundary as having power and meaning. Ultimately, the idea is that he will respond to Mom without having to have a warning and consequence every time.

Internalization is the hope of this process. Mature people understand that when someone asks them to do something that they should, they will do it because they care about the person, or because it's simply the right thing to do. Like very young children, immature people don't respond unless there is the threat of consequences. But over time and withexperience, the process becomes part of the person, and he doesn't require the consequence. Meanwhile, his motives develop from pain avoidance to love, righteousness, and morality.[1]

Determining Appropriate Consequences

An appropriate and well-thought-out consequence can go a very long way in helping the button-pusher become aware, take ownership, change, and grow. The best consequences are a good and deliberate fit to both the situation and the person. There are an almost unlimited number of consequences, as there is no one "right" one. In fact, you may discover that several consequences work in your situation. But I'll list here some principles on how to come up with effective ones. In addition to these, ask around to people who understand these matters. An experienced person can sometimes come up with a new and imaginative way to establish a consequence, which can spur your own creative processes.

Natural Reality

First, consequences that mirror real life are probably preferable, when they are possible. When consequences are close to reality, the button-pusher is more likely to accept that he himself is the cause of his discomfort. He becomes angry and frustrated with himself and takes more ownership to change, so as not to repeat the effect. For example, in the workplace world, a person who is irresponsible with assignments and deadlines should naturally lose promotions, experience discipline and confrontation, and perhaps even lose his job. Though some button-pushers perennially blame their job problems on bad bosses, the company, and the economy, a great number of them change when they experience the real financial and career losses that happen simply because that is the way work operates.

In the relational world, suppose your button-pusher has a pattern of attempting to control you by acting hurt and wounded whenever you don't do what she wants. She pouts and withdraws for extended periods of time until you take the initiative to ask her what is wrong. Then she tells you how deeply your selfishness (more correctly, your freedom) hurts her. If talking is not helping things, a consequence that might be close to natural would be that you will no longer rescue her from her withdrawal. If she takes the first step to go to you and tell you what she is upset about, you will be glad to discuss it with her. But from now on, if she waits for you to take notice of her sadness (which is often a covert anger) and go to her to draw her out, you will not be doing that. So until she takes responsibility, she is removing herself from the relationship and the benefits of the relationship.

Another example concerns the chronically late person who makes meetings and events difficult for everyone, but always has an excuse for it. There are a couple of appropriately natural consequences that might be helpful.

First, everyone in the person's social setting (that is, family and friends) agrees they will not ride with her to an event, but will find their own way and leave on time to get there on time. This is natural because the other people don't want to be late. So she has to drive alone and show up late all by herself, which often is a little embarrassing, as there is no one to distribute the blame to.

A second one is that everyone agrees that life is not suspended until she arrives. That is, you don't wait for her to get to the restaurant to order, you start the Bible study on time, you get the music going at the party, and you throw the first pitch at the ballgame. Again, this is natural, because it's right that the people who took the effort to get there on time shouldn't have to wait for the late person. And it has the effect that she misses out on things she would like to be a part of. Even if she doesn't change, and this is important, *you have still protected and taken ownership of your own time and schedule*. So you are in control of your life, not the button-pusher.

Exceptions to the rule. However, there are times in which natural consequences are not the best thing for the situation. For example, a drug addict risks losing his health and dying from the substance. Obviously, it would not make any sense to say, "Well, maybe that will teach him to stop." A better consequence might be the loss of support from important friends and family members until he agrees to go to rehab.

The most important value to remember concerning the concept of natural consequences is that *it removes you from the parent position with your button-pusher.* The difficult individual often sees the person establishing the consequence as being controlling, mean, or unloving, that is, as an uncaring parent (you) deliberately controlling a child (the button-pusher). This stance disrupts the process of learning, as the individual blames the person, and not himself, for the discomfort. The closer to natural, the more you are out of the way and are less likely to be the object of blame.

In fact, you can even comfort and support the difficult person when he experiences the consequence, if he is able to see his behaviors, and not yours, as the cause of his pain. This is generally down the line in the process, but I have seen lots of times when, for example, a man who alienates his family begins to feel sad and remorseful about what he has done, and his wife is able to support him with grace and love, while still holding on to the consequence until the appropriate time.

The Relational Aspect

Consequences tend to be more productive when they are about *loss of relationship*. The reason for this is that, at the core of our being, we were designed by God to be relational creatures. Your button-pusher needs connection with people for many reasons. Relationship is a lifeline to our existence, and isolation is one of the most profound pains in existence. So when an attachment is jeopardized, it tends to get someone's attention, as it did with Andrea. This is not true in every setting, as is sometimes the case with very detached or self-absorbed individuals, but as a rule, it is the best place to start.

I knew a man who was in love with a woman he had been dating for some time. He was ready to be exclusive with her. She, on the other hand, thought she might be in love with him, but she didn't feel ready to stop dating two other men she was also attached to. The man tried to be patient, but time was passing and she wasn't making any movement in one direction or another. She had feelings for him, but she was unwilling to take responsibility for her problem and look at why she was staying with the other guys. So he finally told her, "I'm moving on. I love you, but I can't stay in limbo. So don't call me unless you are ready to see only me."

She was very angry about this consequence. He really didn't intend it to control her; he was just trying to guard his own heart and life. She called several times to stay in touch, but he stood with the consequence and wouldn't talk to her. Finally, the deprivation caused her to miss him so much that it clarified in her mind that she would rather be without the other two men than without him. She contacted him, hoping he hadn't gotten attached to someone else. Fortunately for her, he hadn't, and ultimately they married. The power of the loss of relationship cannot be overestimated.

Match the Severity

Consequences should not be an underreaction or an overreaction. As is the case with criminal law, the time should match the crime.

If your button-pusher is doing minor things, set a minor consequence. For example, if he doesn't listen to you and watches TV while you are wanting to talk, you might let him know that you may need to take a walk when it's time to help the kids with homework, if he can't spend a little time alone with you.

With more serious infractions, however, you need to be willing to set more severe consequences. If a mate has an affair and is not repentant, you may want to consider a structured therapeutic separation in order to convey the importance and hurt of what she has done. A mildly bothersome button-pusher should not experience the same degree of severity that a very destructive one should.

Use your friends to help here, because it is easy to get things out of proportion due to how close and affected you are by the difficult person. You may have a tendency to go too easy out of your codependence or guilt. On the other hand, your longstanding resentment and hurt may make you tend to swat a fly with a nuclear bomb. Stay in balance, and keep things matched.

Leverage Dependency and Need

This is a very, very, very important consideration for you to think about and act on: *your button-pusher has some sort of dependency on you.* She needs you, or something you have, or something you provide. Otherwise, with the conflicts you have, why is she still in the relationship?

This is so important because you may have power that you are not aware of in the relationship. Having said that, remember it is not about having the power to control, fix, or hurt her. It is having and using your power to leverage a consequence that could make a real difference in influencing her to change. You matter at some level, and that has meaning for her.

I cannot tell you how many times I have talked to a spouse on the radio program who is in a very troubled marriage and says, *He won't do anything I ask when I say I want the problem to stop. There's nothing I can do that will make a difference.* Then, as we explore the marriage, we almost always find something that she can use that matters to him and could help things. One answer, for example, for the problem of the wife who will not stop criticizing her husband no matter what, is to ultimately not be present when she is doing it. The chronically critical person needs someone to listen and absorb what she is saying, and not being present can often help get her attention that there are better ways to relate. Another example regarding the husband who has a pattern of being indifferent to his wife's feelings and life is to require talking, closeness, and interest in order for her to feel warm and safe enough to have relations with him. This is not being deceptive, since it is acting on a reality about how sexuality and relationship interact: the emotional union was designed by God to lead to the sexual union, not the reverse.

This last example must be thought through carefully, and with spiritually mature friends. First Corinthians 7:4–5 teaches that husbands and wives are not to deprive each other of sexual relations, in order to protect the marriage from temptation. This is an important biblical principle. However, if the wife is being pressured to have relations when she is uncared for or even mistreated by her husband, something very wrong is going on. So, get good feedback on this, and be sure to understand any passage in the context of the entire counsel of Scripture. For example, the husband's responsibility to abide in a deep and self-sacrificing love for his wife must also be part of your thinking (Ephesians 5:25, 33). Ultimately, sex is a gift and not a weapon. No spouse should demand it when love and care are not present; no spouse should withdraw it to get re-venge on or punish the other.

When you understand the leverage you have, it also helps you emotionally. As we have discussed, people in a relationship with a button-pusher often feel great degrees of helplessness, powerless-ness, and frustration. They feel shut out and that no decisions they can make will make any difference. Becoming aware that you have power and leverage can go a long way to help you feel like you can do some things to help.

Things to Consider

Here is a brief listing of some things you may unknowingly possess which you may be able to use. Some of these things will not really matter to your button-pusher. But some of them, and others which aren't listed here, should. Take advantage of the reality that you are probably providing some things that, though he may not admit it, he genuinely needs and wants.

Remember to keep your motive pure here. It's not about getting back at your button-pusher, or showing him how he makes you feel. It's about getting his attention so that he draws a connection be-tween his behavior and his discomfort, and makes the necessary changes. And, if he changes, make sure he gets these benefits back, wholeheartedly and generously, at the appropriate time:

- Acceptance of his faults
- Warmth toward her
- Emotional presence with him
- Affirmation of the relationship
- Encouragement to help her move ahead

- Support for his struggles
- Affection for her
- Interest in his world and life
- Physical presence in the room with her
- Empathy for his pain
- Cooking, cleaning, organizing, or doing chores
- Fixing things around the house
- Making the home a pleasant environment
- Attending to her felt needs
- Space and quietness around him
- Respect for what is respectable in her
- Spontaneity to give him life
- Entertainment to help her enjoy things
- Humor to help him with perspective
- Dependability to give her someone to rely on
- Structure to help organize him
- Task abilities to be available to her
- Help in providing friendships and social activities that are enjoyable
- Practical thinking to help him with dreams and ideas
- Financial support and resourcing
- Planning to give focus to her future
- Wisdom to give him direction

- Feedback to help her stay on track
- Insight to help him be aware of situations
- Depth to bring her into the inner world of life
- Creativity to help him see things in a different light
- Solutions that she has not seen to her life problems
- A social system and setting that matters to him
- Spirituality, which grounds her to God and her faith
- The cultural tradition of marriage, which anchors people
- Family ties, which give her a sense of rootedness and belonging
- Living together in the home, which keeps him from loneliness

A button-pusher is often dependent on the other individual, because the world would not put up with his tendencies. So she serves as protection, comfort, a buffer, and a sanctuary for him so that he does not have to face his failure to adapt to the world. The most aloof, strong-appearing, self-sufficient person often hides loneliness, fear, and an inability to make and keep friends. I have seen so many of these people begin to crumble when the things they depended on in the other person were no longer available for the right amount of time. They sometimes get depressed—the kind of depression psychologists call a *productive depression*. This means the depression is the first step of becoming real, facing issues, and changing. Don't rescue your button-pusher from this depression if it will help him grow. If you remove some of these buffers, he may have to experience the loneliness that will help him see what he is doing to you, himself, and the relationship.

So you may need to think with your friends which ones of these items on the list will matter most to your button-pusher, and tell him at some point something like this:

"If you don't stop doing X, you will lose some benefits of being with me. I will withhold them to keep myself safe; because I don't feel close or loved by you; and because I hope you will get the message that I am serious about your behavior, and I will not tolerate it."

In your careful use of power with your button-pusher, ". . . .be shrewd as serpents and innocent as doves" (Matthew 10:16 NASB).

THE LOGISTICS OF CONSEQUENCES

In a word, the more specific, the better. That applies to what the consequence is, when it applies, to what level it applies, and what the conditions are for it to be removed. Be as clear and unmistakable as possible. You don't want any confusion to pop up later and be blamed for being too severe or withholding or unfair.

It is unfortunate that you need to be this specific and exacting, but this is based on the reality of the nature of being in a relationship with a button-pusher. Remember that you didn't start off in the relationship thinking that you had to keep specific boundaries and limits. And hopefully, if your button-pusher responds to the pressure, you can let go of them at some safe point. Good and healthy relationships are different in nature; they are more driven by the spirit of the law than the letter of the law. If you tell your friend that he hurt your feelings, you talk, he apologizes and changes, and the relationship moves on. You know he will hold up his end of things.

But good relationships are built on dependency and trust. Relationships with button-pushers often have trust problems, and the person must depend on himself rather than the other individual. *With a button-pusher, trust is often a goal to be worked toward, not an assumption to make.* Because of that, you have to impose the law rather than the spirit until things change and you can trust his intents and motives. As the Bible says, "The law is not made for a righteous person, but for those who are lawless and rebellious" (1 Timothy 1:9 NASB).

So, continuing the example of the angry husband from chapter 9, you might say something like this:

"I went to Nicole's when you blew up, but it didn't seem to change things with you. So I will be spending a couple of evenings a week with friends and my support group, so that I can manage staying in the relationship. Weekends, I will spend most of my time out of the house or with friends. I won't be going on any social outings with you because I don't trust that you won't get enraged again. If you take responsibility for the anger, I would like to get back to spending more time with you, but not until then."

Follow Through

There is no substitute for following through with a consequence. This is the action that makes your words have meaning and substance to your button-pusher, rather than nagging that he simply ignores and dismisses. It is when you walk your talk.

There is no real rocket science to following through. It is more a matter of determining if you have the necessary support, resources, emotional wherewithal, and courage to go through with it.

Establish and plan for your resources. If this is a major intervention, surround yourself with help. Get involved with a church that is into process and supporting people in trouble. Find friends and helpers who understand these matters. Read books on the subject. I have seen some churches that were such a resource in a button-pushing relationship that the board of elders would visit a home just to confront and deal with a marriage issue that was in crisis.

Stay out of dependence on the difficult person, and stay connected to others. Don't think that because you are fed up today, that your determination and commitment today is a guarantee that you will hold to the consequence tomorrow and the next day. Remember that your button-pusher is not the only one with dependencies. You are likely to also miss the good things you value about him. And the more you need things from the button-pusher, the less likely you will be able to follow through. Get your needs for warmth, structure, support, and validation met through your support system. Then, if the person begins withdrawing emotional supplies from you, you have somewhere to go to be replenished and strengthened. Make sure that your safe and sane relationships are aware of all this, and are on call for you in moments of weakness when you want to cave in and lift the consequence.

Deal with emotional issues such as guilt and codependence. Setting consequences is a new world for many people. They have never done it before, or at least very well, and it is strange for them. Often, emotional issues will arise to detract from the focus. If you have a pattern of threatening and not following through, you may have to deal with guilt, loneliness, doubt, fear of separation, and a host of other emotions. Guilty feelings that you are being cruel may come up. Or codependence, a feeling that you should rescue the person with your love, may emerge. Pay attention to these issues, and keep them processed in relationship. Heal from them and give them a place to go so that you can stay grounded in reality about your situation.

Normalize escalation. Do not be surprised if your difficult person escalates, that is, increases her problem behavior, initially. That is pretty normal and to be expected. Keep making sure that your supportive people think you're on the right track, and stay steady. The escalation is a sign that something is happening and changing, hopefully in time, something good for both of you.

Most of the time, escalation is not a thought-out or deliberate

156

strategy designed to get you off track. Rather, it tends to be, simply put, a tantrum. Like a three-year-old, she is angrily protesting something she doesn't enjoy or like. Often, button-pushers never went through a childhood in which they received consistent, loving, strict, and appropriate limits. So now they are three-year-olds in an adult body! The process you are helping to occur is for them to work through the escalation, realize the reality that they can't do or say anything they please, grieve and be sad over what has happened, and begin to grow up inside. That is what resolves the child's developmental tantrum stage, and it may be a stage that your person missed the first time around.

I am not saying that escalation is fun. Sometimes it can even be dangerous. For example, if an angry person gets truly abusive or violent, you must protect yourself and bring in more resources. But if you can safely stay with the limits, the escalation often begins to subside over time as the person moves more into acceptance and grief about letting go of her own omnipotence.

Keep as warm and "for" the person as possible during escalation. Don't get into punitive or harsh words, for she will be more likely to attribute the problem to your meanness, and not her own behavior. Say things like, "I'm sorry it's so painful for you right now. I don't enjoy this either, and I want to get back to us. But with you as angry and out of control as you are, I need to keep my distance and the limit, until you choose to change things."

Tighten? Loosen? Change?

It is likely that you will need to keep monitoring and re-evaluating your boundaries and consequences. This is a fluid process, and people change and shift. Most of the time, the button-pusher will not stop the bad behavior the first time you establish the consequence, though it happens sometimes. Don't be rigidly locked into one approach. Keep tweaking it until you find the best combination.

Tightening. You may find, for example, that your consequence doesn't really matter to the person, or that it isn't strict enough. After a reasonable period of time, determined by you and experienced people, if you see no change, or if escalation doesn't resolve at all, a different consequence may be necessary. This may seem somewhat detached, as if the person is a research project. But the reality is that you need thoughtfulness, wisdom, and help in order to create the best possible context for your button-pusher to change and begin to grow. It is, ultimately, deeply personal.

I have a friend who was running his family's finances into the ground. He was in the habit of making very risky investments with money they couldn't afford to lose, and without a lot of experience behind him. He blew off his wife's and friends' warnings, thinking that they were just too conservative to get the real picture about the opportunities. The first consequence his wife established was that she began withdrawing emotionally from him and spending time away from him, as she was afraid of him and didn't trust who he was. Then, when that didn't work, she asked him to go to a support group for feedback, which he did.

However, after a period of time, it became apparent that his financial habits weren't changing, and he could withstand her distance and the group's influence. The wife then consulted with some people and finally asked him to move out, away from her and the kids, until he began to be more financially responsible. This mattered to him. He had a strong value for being with the family, and the isolation, loneliness, and lack of warmth were quite distressing to him. Though he continued to blame her for some time for being unloving, she kept that tighter consequence. After a period of time, he began to agree to submit his finances to others in his church who would help him get back in balance.

If your consequence (or consequences) is in the right area that matters to your button-pusher, there is a principle here: *Keep it just strict enough to see movement and change, and no stricter.* Don't be punitive, vengeful, or controlling. Give as much grace as you can within the stricter limit. And, by the same token, if your limit is too severe, and reasonable people think you are overreacting, be willing to lighten up. The important thing is for the difficult person to be in enough discomfort to change, but not in so much that he may be discouraged from the process and give up in hopelessness.

When to let up. How do you determine when it is time to release the consequence? You don't want to stop it just because the person says "OK, I'll change." Nor do you want to if he makes some initial response that doesn't show a pattern. Here are some tips:

❖ *When change goes along with words.*

You must insist that the person actually do things differently: start being more responsible, stop the criticism, end the drinking, or whatever. It is a good start if he agrees and apologizes. He may even mean it. But usually, he does not have the internal structure or tools to actually change. The result is that the person ends the consequence because she misses him and believes his good intentions. This is one of the biggest problems I see in follow-through. Words are important, but they require a change.

❖ *When change occurs over a period of time.*

Time is a valuable resource. A person can make lots of healthy-appearing changes very quickly. Look at how people act on a first date! But—and remembering this can really help you—*character will always emerge over time.* That is just the way God made us. Who we are, with our flaws and deficits, will eventually come out in the passage of time. True change will stand the test. This doesn't mean there won't be slip-ups and regressions. Have grace and patience with them if the person is truly trying to change. But talk to people with experience in these matters, who have seen many similar situations, and come up with a time period of sustained change that indicates that the person is truly doing things differently.

Some button-pushers with a more deceptive character will change and then, once they are back in the relationship, revert to their old ways. Inside themselves, they didn't change because it was the right thing to do, but to get the person to drop the limit. If you observe this, it isn't the end of the world. It is simply more valuable diagnostic information about him. Go ahead and re-establish consequences. And this time, with mentoring, you may want to change or lengthen the requirements.

❖ *When there is evidence of heart change.*

This is a very good indicator. When the person is sorry he got caught, that's normal. When he is sorry he has to endure consequences, that is good. But when he is sorry about the pain he has caused you and others, that is good news. Look for true and authentic remorse and contrition.

❖ *When he gets into the growth process for himself.*

Give a lot of credence to your difficult person if he begins looking at his issues and gets into some structure for spiritual and personal growth, such as a group, a pastor, or therapy. Not only might it be a sign that he is wanting to truly grow, not just change his behavior, but also now you have more people helping support, monitor, and evaluate progress.

❖ *When people you trust are OK with it.*

Stay in touch with the safe and sane relationships who are for you, for the button-pusher, and for the relationship. They may see green lights you are missing, or red lights you don't see. Listen to them and get their perspective.

❖ *When God speaks to you.*

Stay attuned to the Holy Spirit and constantly ask God for guidance and direction. He knows your button-pusher's heart better than anyone, and he will help you know when things should change.

GOD AND CONSEQUENCES

One of the biggest problems in setting and enforcing consequences is the concern that we have mentioned, that you are being unloving and hurtful with your person. It is likely that when you set limits for the first time, and begin to follow through, the button-pusher may blame you. Or friends and family may not support you. And your own conscience may attack you. Certainly it is wise to always question and review your motives and how you are handling the relationship. But let God, reality, and safe and healthy relationships guide you, not the protests of those who do not understand what is going on.

It can be very helpful to know and adopt the stance that God himself takes about the limits and consequences he has had to keep with his own people. He does not relish in our pain. It is not fun for him. But it has a design, a purpose, and a hope: *that we will simply return to him*. Returning to relationship, and to his ways, is all that matters, because if those happen, pretty much everything else in life ends up falling into place. If the difficulty we experience finally gets through to us that we are better off coming back to him, he welcomes us, and it has all been worthwhile:

> And when you and your children return to the Lord your God and obey him with all your heart and with all your soul according to everything I command you today, then the Lord your God will restore your fortunes and have compassion on you and gather you again from all the nations where he scattered you. (Deuteronomy 30:2–3)

Think about these actions with your difficult person in the same way: You simply want her to *return to the paths of love and responsibility with you*. When she does, you are more than willing to restore your heart, and all the other benefits of the relationship, to her. That is not punishment. That is love.

RESOURCE #7: THE PROCESS

I WAS SPEAKING AT A CONFERENCE on solving relationship
problems. During a break, a pastor who works with couples
came up to me and asked, "What do you think about temporary
separations to solve a serious relationship issue?"

"Maybe; it depends," I said. "What is your understanding of a
temporary separation?"

He said, "Well, when the two people stay away from each other.
Like in a marriage, one moves out. Or in a friendship, they don't
contact each other for a while."

"Anything else involved?" I said.

He thought a minute. "Not really. I guess to me, it's like a time-
out for grownups where they both calm down and think about what
they have done, and get back together."

"Well, with your description of a temporary separation, I would
say that it's minimally useful, maybe even useless, especially given
the trouble people have to go through to pull it off."

He said, "What do you mean?"

I said, "Because time away isn't the entire healing process. It's part of it. But basically *time in separation only serves to hold the elements of healing in one place.* For a separation to work, it's not the absence of being around each other's toxicity, or whatever we want to call it. It is much more the presence of the growth activities. Separation isn't a time-out. It is, in fact, a very, very busy and intentional period in which lots of important things are going on."

Your relationship with the button-pusher may be far from having to consider separation. Regardless, there is a process of time that you need to know how to use to your advantage. Your connection with the difficult person has taken time to develop into what it is now. Whatever has been making you crazy probably didn't happen immediately. And it will take time for your approach to be structured in such a way that your button-pusher experiences what he needs to experience, in order to be willing to make the necessary and required changes.

This is your seventh resource: *You are a guardian of the process that is going on over time with your relationship.*

The Right Kind of Time Is on Your Side

Time alone does not heal or change a person, any more than time heals an infection not treated with antibiotics. Time all by itself actually works for the button-pusher's ends. If you don't like her deceptiveness and simply wait for her to change, she has no real pressure or influence on her to do anything about it. She can wait you out, and experience no discomfort.

But the right kind of time can be very productive. Time that is filled with your own growth work. Time that encompasses prayer and dependence on God to get through to your button-pusher; with the right kinds of talks, such as we dealt with in chapter 9; and with the right kinds of boundaries and consequences we discussed in chapter 10. This time-plus-action applies the needed antibiotics to bring about the differences you are looking for.

So take an active approach to time rather than a passive "waiting" stance, which generally is based on fear and discouragement rather than faith anyway. Use the time to monitor a process that your button-pusher is continually exposed to and experiencing. The infections in her mind and soul are constantly being bombarded by the medicine you bring through our seven resources. As we said earlier, she is outmanned and outgunned by God and reality. She certainly is free to frustrate the process, but it should not be easy for her to live that way. Ultimately, you would like her to choose righteousness and change because it is less painful, and brings her more benefits, than the darkness and blindness in which she currently keeps her residence.

Here are some aspects of using the process of time to keep the seven elements involved as you help the button-pusher.

Persistence

Remember the "one time should do it" mentality we dealt with in chapter 3? This is the thinking that if you have told your button-pusher to stop whatever he is doing, or if you have set a limit once, he should come around; and if he doesn't, none of this works and you'd better try something else.

If you have concluded that, you are absolutely right. It doesn't work, and shouldn't. But the "it" is not what we have been presenting in this book. An approach to a person with low ownership over his life and behavior should never be looked at as a one-time event, but as *a process: a period of many intentional events which are integrated together to create an environment that promotes and pressures the person to change.* You combine antibiotics, rest, fluids, and other things to create the context of growth.

This requires persistence. Your button-pusher may honestly not understand what you are asking the first time. Or he may play dumb or ignore you so that you will give up. He may not believe you are serious. He may think he can wait you out, or intimidate or manipulate you. He may counterattack and blame you for everything.

You must hang in there. You may have to repeat your talks and conversations. You might have to restate the boundaries. You are almost guaranteed to experience more than one trial of establishing and following through on the consequences. Get used to that, and be patient. Remember how long it took for you yourself to get the picture on something you needed to change, and how long it took to change.

Persistence and diligence are the type of attributes that don't get a lot of press. They aren't very sexy. However, very few worthwhile things in life happen without them. All the talent, creativity, and good intentions in the world will be stillborn unless someone is around who can plod along, faithfully executing what needs to be done: "The plans of the diligent lead to profit as surely as haste leads to poverty" (Proverbs 21:5). The guys on the offensive line in football don't get a lot of glory. But the wise quarterback lets them know, over and over again, how much he values and appreciates their protection of his body!

I have a friend, George, whose button-pusher is Sharon, his wife. For years, Sharon has had a strong tendency to blame and criticize him constantly. Little things, big things, things that he has done wrong, and things that he hasn't—all have been fair game for her. George has certainly not been perfect, but in no way has his punishment fit his crimes. George's marriage has been an illustration of Proverbs 21:9: "Better to live on a corner of the roof than share a house with a quarrelsome wife."

George began living the principles in this book with Sharon. One thing he began to say to her was "I want to know when your feedback is true about me. But when it isn't, or when you are what I consider inappropriate, I'll go to another room or the backyard and read the paper until you can speak without being so critical." Sharon would lash out, and George would say, "OK, I'm going now." And she would be alone in the room with no one to hear her criticisms.

Sharon was pretty set in her position and resisted seeing that any of this was her fault. It wasn't bad enough in George's mind to do anything drastic like leave or call someone. And there was enough good in the marriage that he liked the positive parts of the relationship. So he figured, *This may never change her, but at least it will keep me sane.* And he would repeat the above statements and leave the room over and over again. He had settled in his mind that this was the way it was. Everybody has problems, and if she never changed, it was still an OK life.

But she did change. It took a lot of repetition and adherence to the boundary. And eventually Sharon realized George wasn't being mean. He wasn't angry. He returned in a good mood and was pleasant with her. This finally got through to her, and she softened up and became less strident. Persistence, patience, and diligence are your friends with the button-pusher.

Deal with the Victim-Persecutor Dynamic

A common theme in many button-pushing relationships is the victim-persecutor dynamic. This refers to what often happens when the button-pusher is confronted or has a consequence established with him. Instead of repenting, apologizing, feeling remorse, or, best and highest of all, showing gratitude, the difficult person will feel that he is being victimized, and that the other person is persecuting him. This can derail the process of confronting or setting boundaries, which is sometimes the intent.

When your button-pusher says, "You have really wounded me," it often evokes concern or guilt feelings that have nothing to do with the reality.

While we are always to be open to the possibility that our words and actions are unkind or inappropriate, look for a particular pattern here, to determine what is going on: What causes your button-pusher to scream *victim?* If it is unkindness or unfairness, change what you are doing. *But if it tends to be that you have simply disagreed, confronted, said no, or set a limit, that is suspect.* When the trigger is truth, reality, or consequences, there is a possibility that your difficult person is experiencing *truth itself as the persecution.* The roots of this may be deep, and often are the result of a lack of healthy experiences with confrontation so that the button-pusher has no skills or abilities to see truth as his friend. *For him, grace and getting his way equal love, and truth and confrontation equal hate.*

If you see this in the process, do not ignore it, for it doesn't tend to resolve on its own. It is a character issue, and must be addressed. Say something like this:

"It is hard to work out problems with you, because it seems that most of the time when I tell you a reality, you think I am being mean to you. I'd like to work on this so that you can feel OK with my feedback. Then maybe we can get back to a good relationship that solves problems for both of us."

Sometimes, making this an area of focus can help your button-pusher to develop what is called an observing ego, the ability to look at oneself objectively and make value judgments on what one is doing. With the power of self-observation, the person can learn to safely see how easily he falls into the victim-persecutor dance and begins to take ownership of his feelings when he is confronted.

Know What to Do When You See Results

It really happens: this oven of growth can actually bake a changing person! However, you need to know what to do when you see things change so that you can increase the likelihood of more good stuff.

Show appreciation. First, get happy and convey that happiness! From God's perspective, when someone changes his ways, there is a party in heaven: ". . . There is rejoicing in the presence of the angels of God over one sinner who repents" (Luke 15:10). Your button-pusher probably had to restrain or risk in some new and uncomfortable ways to change. Let her know how much you appreciate the effort. More than anything, go back to the relational context. Show her how the love and connectedness, affirmation, respect, or whatever she values in the relationship, are now more forthcoming because she is making good moves and choices. You must always temper this with the reality that one change may not mean that the consequences are dropped, as we discussed in chapter 10. But there is a lot you can do to reinforce change so that it is likely to continue.

I was doing marital counseling with a couple in which the marriage was struggling, largely because the husband was very defensive and unwilling to admit faults and weaknesses. His wife had just burnt out on always being the bad guy, and they were in trouble. After some work and focus on this, one day he said to her, "I think I have been screwing up with the way I have been treating you." It wasn't an eloquent confession, but it was heartfelt, and I believed him. His wife was awesome. She looked at him and said, "Yes, you have been. But it really helps for you to say that. Thanks." She didn't come all the way back to him emotionally, but you could tell the temperature between them had warmed up. He looked different, too, like a guy who was proud of himself for taking a first right step.

Breakthroughs and Gradual Shifts

Sometimes button-pushers have breakthrough experiences in which something gets through to them in a dramatic and powerful way, and they understand at a deep level what they have been doing to themselves and to people they care about. It can happen in many ways: a confrontation can cause a flash of insight; God can speak to her in some mysterious fashion; a warning or consequence can produce a quick effect; a third party's appeal can touch her. These are mountaintop experiences, and are often defining moments in a person's life.

Most of the time, these breakthrough experiences do not occur in a vacuum. Often they are the visible result of a great deal of invisible growth that has been going on through the steady application of these resources. Over time, the forces for health converge to help him see what he is doing. The breakthrough event is the last piece in the puzzle, and helps everything come together.

A man I worked with blamed his Internet porn addiction on his wife, his stress, and anyone who crossed him. He was not close to admitting he needed help until one day, in a conversation, he realized how hurtful he had been to his wife. He began to sob uncontrollably with such remorse over what he had done to her, and ended up almost in a fetal position on the floor. He was never the same again, and has changed in many profound ways. But, if you were to look at his life in the months and years before that experience, you would see that people had been praying; friends had been steadily confronting him in love; he had encountered relational and other losses due to the habit; and his wife had stayed with him, though she did not feel safe with him. Breakthroughs are sometimes miraculous in nature, and are sometimes no mystery at all.

However, breakthroughs are not the only way that change occurs in your button-pusher. Sometimes small and gradual changes will become apparent. Though not as dramatic, these are as much cause for rejoicing as intense flashes of insight. Sometimes an irresponsible adult child will be thankful instead of demanding. A moody friend will ask for help. A controlling boss will be more supportive and relational in small ways. A spiritualizing person at church will admit that she struggles in some area.

Sometimes the gradual changes are just behaviors, such as an angry person restraining the impulse to blow up, or a spendaholic showing a decrease in spending over a few months. In these sorts of cases, the behavioral patterns may show up even before the person admits they have been out of control. This often means that the pressures are working, and the person is responding because at some level they want to avoid the pain that their behavior causes, even before they can tell themselves or anyone else that they are at fault. Insight is sometimes the result of the cure rather than the cause. It is very important to know this, so that if you see gradual behavioral shifts without confession or admission, you won't be disappointed. It is a good sign, and often the confession follows as the person continues to grow and becomes safe and humble enough to face the truth.

Whether you see gradual or intense changes, change is good. Without being patronizing, recognize the shifts in your difficult person and work with your support team on what seems to be working and why. Keep the program going.

Grief and Adaptation

During the process, you will most likely be changed as much as you wish your button-pusher will be, and sometimes more. One likely change for you is the need to come to terms with your own grief, and to learn how to adapt to what is real. This is because the process is almost always accompanied by failures, regressions, escalations, and stuckness. It may be that the changes are coming at a much slower rate than you wanted. That is a matter of adapting and coping, as well as facing the sad feelings of the loss.

It is always a possibility also that your difficult person may not make any changes over time, no matter how you approach her. That can certainly be a serious disappointment for you and for the relationship. Be prepared to face your sadness and the lost dreams you have had for her.

The ability to grieve and adapt works for you even when the button-pusher is not responding. It allows you to accept and process through what is real and actual so that you can adjust what is the next best thing to do. Your odds of seeing change in the button-pusher are increased if you allow the sad feelings to keep you attuned to what is true in the relationship.

Though it would be a huge loss for your button-pusher to stay unmoved and unchanged through this entire endeavor, it is not the end of life. Life can be a very good thing for you, independent of your person's progress or lack of progress.

In chapter 6 I talked about dealing with the dependencies you may have on your button-pusher. To wish and desire his change is very different from depending on his change to have a fulfilling life. In fact, if you have this sort of dependency in a good relationship, you risk messing it up. Depend on God, his process of growth, and a safe and loving support system. From that strong vantage point, keep caring for your difficult person. And hope in God's interest in bringing him back to himself.

I have a friend whose wife is a very difficult person. She is quite unhappy and negative, and sort of infects other people with the disease. The two of them have been married a long time. My friend has faithfully loved her, though it has not been easy. And he has used his resources to promote change, sometimes a lot, and sometimes not very much. So far, she has not seemed to respond.

But if you were to interview him and ask him about his life, I am certain that this man would say, *I have a good life*. He does not feel like she has robbed his life of happiness. He has worked a lot on the ability to detach from her hurtful parts so that he doesn't get very wounded by her anymore. He enjoys the good parts of her and the good times they do have. He has a deep faith, and is involved in his church and helping the less fortunate. He has good and sound friends, and lots of interests in life. He has let go of what he can't have from her, but he keeps the tension of letting himself hope that there still might be change. You never know. Only God does.

When people ask me, *When do I give up hope on my button-pusher?* I tell them, "Never, as long as they are alive. Give up the demand and the requirement that they must change. But keep hoping, and continue doing all of the things today that could make a difference tomorrow." That is the way to live in the kind of hope that God provides: "May the God of hope fill you with all joy and peace as you trust in him, so that you may overflow with hope by the power of the Holy Spirit" (Romans 15:13).

CONCLUSION:
RELATIONSHIPS REVISITED

HAVING A DIFFICULT RELATIONSHIP tends to reduce life, and reduce ourselves, to the bare essentials. Living in the tension between loving someone deeply and yet embracing his freedom not to return your love, helps us to understand what is really important, and what is less so. What truly matters in the scheme of things except those great themes of life such as God, relationship, love, truth, growth, freedom, and making a return? I cannot think of much more than these few.

In that spirit, learn to thank God for using our button-pusher to render things down so much that we are preserved from the futility of spending our days roaming the earth, distracted from the people and activities that should fill our lives with purpose and meaning.

Having said that, it is helpful to revisit the entire concept of relationship as it relates to you and your difficult person. He is in your life, and you are in his, for a purpose, and that purpose is always about growth and redemption. You are to serve his growth, and he yours. Do not make the mistake of looking upon him as a curse to be borne, a burden to be survived, a problem to be solved, or, worst of all, a project to be completed. He, like yourself, needs grace and forgiveness, as well as limits and consequences.

All the resources that you bring to bear upon the relationship's repair and change do have great power and potential, for they are given by God, who desires that all of us return to him and grow into his image. So keep your mind and your vision on what was probably the original hope you had for the connection: that you can someday enjoy this person's presence and companionship without having to continue warning, confronting, guarding, and limiting. Ultimately, move toward a relationship which, when the time and circumstances are right, is marked and defined more by trust and grace than by strategy and pressure.

When an infant is born, the first thing she sees is her mother's face as Mom smiles at her baby and welcomes her to the land of life. The baby drinks in the safety and warmth she feels there. In the adult years, when two people marry or establish a deep friendship, they look forward to those times in which they can sit quietly together, needing no words, for they are attuned to each other's presence. And in the last moments of our lives, all of us would desire to be surrounded by those people who have mattered most to us, holding our hand and conveying their endearments as they usher us into the hands of God. His design is that your relationship would grow and transform into one that can distribute that kind of care and love mutually between you two.

It ultimately derives from the Source of all reconciliation and growth, and that is God himself. He never ceases striving, in so many different ways, to bring a difficult and wayward race to communion with himself: "I will walk among you and be your God, and you will be my people" (Leviticus 26:12). As you walk in faith to change and grow in your own life, and to help your difficult person change, you are taking your place in God's grand plan and design. It is a good way to live a life.

May God bless you.

ENDNOTES

Chapter 1

1. *Raising Great Kids* (Grand Rapids, Mich.: Zondervan, 1999).
2. My book *Hiding from Love* (Grand Rapids, Mich.: Zondervan, 1991) deals with this process in detail.

Chapter 3

1. Matthew 23:23.
2. Henry Cloud's *Changes That Heal: How to Understand Your Past to Ensure a Healthier Future* (Grand Rapids, Mich.: Zondervan, 2003) has an excellent treatment of the splitting of grace and truth.
3. If you find that you do not choose very safe people, Henry's and my book *Safe People: How to Find Relationships That Are Good for You and Avoid Those That Aren't* (Grand Rapids, Mich.: Zondervan, 1995) explains how to discern safe from unsafe people.

Chapter 5

1. See *Boundaries: When to Say Yes and When to Say No to Take Control of Your Life* (Grand Rapids, Mich.: Zondervan, 1991) by Henry Cloud and me about these and other laws of relationship and responsibility.

FOR FURTHER READING

Cloud, Dr. Henry. *Changes That Heal. How to Understand Your Past to Ensure a Healthier Future*. Grand Rapids, Mich.: Zondervan, 1992.

Cloud, Dr. Henry and Dr. John Townsend. *Boundaries: When to Say Yes, When to Say No to Take Control of Your Life*. Grand Rapids, Mich.: Zondervan, 1992.

Cloud and Townsend. *Boundaries Face to Face: How to Have That Difficult Conversation You've Been Avoiding*. Zondervan, 2003.

Cloud and Townsend. *Boundaries in Dating*. Grand Rapids, Mich.: Zondervan, 2000.

Cloud and Townsend. *Boundaries in Marriage*. Grand Rapids, Mich.: Zondervan, 1999.

Cloud and Townsend. *Boundaries with Kids*. Grand Rapids, Mich.: Zondervan, 1998.

Cloud and Townsend. *God Will Make a Way: What to Do When You Don't Know What to Do*. Nashville, Tenn.: Integrity, 2002.

Cloud and Townsend. *How People Grow: What the Bible Reveals about Personal Growth*. Grand Rapids, Mich.: Zondervan, 2001.

FOR FURTHER READING

Cloud and Townsend. *Making Small Groups Work: What Every Small Group Leader Needs to Know*. Grand Rapids, Mich.: Zondervan, 2003.

Cloud and Townsend. *The Mom Factor: Dealing with the Mother You Had, Didn't Have, or Still Contend With*. Grand Rapids, Mich.: Zondervan, 1996.

Cloud and Townsend. *Raising Great Kids: A Comprehensive Guide to Parenting with Grace and Truth*. Grand Rapids, Mich.: Zondervan, 1999.

Cloud and Townsend. *Safe People: How to Find Relationships That Are Good for You and Avoid Those That Aren't*. Grand Rapids, Mich.: Zondervan, 1995.

Cloud and Townsend. *12 "Christian" Beliefs that Can Drive You Crazy*. Grand Rapids, Mich.: Zondervan, 1995.

Townsend, Dr. John. *Hiding from Love: How to Change the Withdrawal Patterns That Isolate and Imprison You*. Grand Rapids, Mich.: Zondervan, 1996.

DON'T YOU HATE IT WHEN YOU'VE DONE EVERYTHING YOU KNOW TO DO AND YOU STILL CAN'T MAKE IT WORK?

—⌘—

In *God Will Make a Way*, Dr. Henry Cloud and Dr. John Townsend present eight fascinating and persuasive principles that demonstrate how God moves in difficult situations. Then they show the principles at work in twelve key areas of life such as personal goals, sex, dating, conflict, parenting, fear, destructive habits and more. You'll have the tools you need to regain control of your life, make your relationships better and satisfy your spiritual hunger.

Whether you're currently in a "fix" or just looking for more out of life, this book is about how God shows up in ways you never dreamed possible.

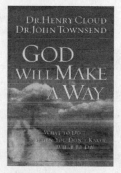

God Will Make a Way

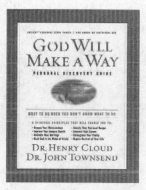

God Will Make a Way
Personal Discovery Guide

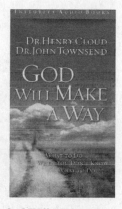

God Will Make a Way
Audio Book

AVAILABLE WHEREVER BOOKS ARE SOLD

WHAT TO DO WHEN YOU DON'T KNOW
WHAT TO DO

———❧———

The perfect gift!

According to best-selling authors Drs. Henry Cloud and John Townsend, when you find yourself lost and confused, you are ready to experience God like never before. In this beautifully designed gift-sized book, the eight principles found in *God Will Make a Way* are culled down to the basics—basics that will simply change your life.

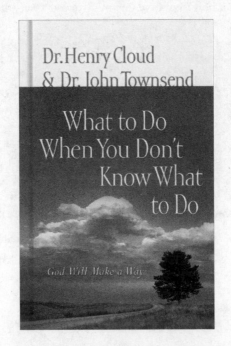